BALTIMORE

PHOTOGRAPHY AND TEXT BY MIDDLETON EVANS

MIDDLETON PRESS, INC. • BALTIMORE, MARYLAND

CONTENTS

Above: Reflections of the setting sun accent the stark geometry of Baltimore's Inner Harbor.

Page 1: True to form, the swift clipper ship Pride of Baltimore II slices across the Chesapeake Bay.

Page 2: The Washington Monument greets northbound motorists passing through Mount Vernon Place, old Baltimore at its best.

Page 3: The 28-story 100 East Pratt, with its evocative steel canopy, and cascading waterfalls at the McKeldin Fountain testify to a vibrant revitalization of downtown Baltimore.

International Standard Book Number: 0-9620806-3-2
Library of Congress Catalog Card Number: 92-85433
Copyright ©: Middleton Evans, 1992
No portion of this book, photography or text, may be
reproduced without the permission of the publisher:
Middleton Press, Inc.
7801 York Road - Suite 145
Baltimore, Maryland 21204
Telephone: (410) 821-1090

Printing: Garamond Pridemark Press • Baltimore, Maryland
Color Separations: Baltimore Color Plate • Baltimore, Maryland
Binding: Advantage Book Binding • Glen Burnie, Maryland
Typography: Art Comp & Design Company • Timonium, Maryland
Book Design: Middleton Evans
Editor: Elizabeth A. Hughes
First Edition

Towering 230-foot cranes, billed as among the world's fastest, service an Evergreen Line ship at Seagirt Marine

Terminal, Baltimore's state-of-the-art container facility, opened in 1989 by the Maryland Port Administration.

A tight pack of thoroughbreds rounds the first turn nose-to-nose during a thrilling race at Pimlico Race Track;

the Sport of Kings is one of the thriving sports which feeds Baltimore's enthusiasm for competition.

Inner Harbor guests are treated to the soothing sounds of the Baltimore Symphony Orchestra ... celebrated as

"Baltimore's other major league team" — during the Tenth Anniversary Party for Harborplace in 1990.

Grand old maples herald the glory of autumn along a favorite path at Robert E. Lee Memorial Park, 500 acres of

wilderness surrounding Lake Roland, where Baltimoreans can escape the stresses of life in a big city.

East of the Inner Harbor, an older Baltimore recalls a working-class city... proud of its ethnic heritage, bustling

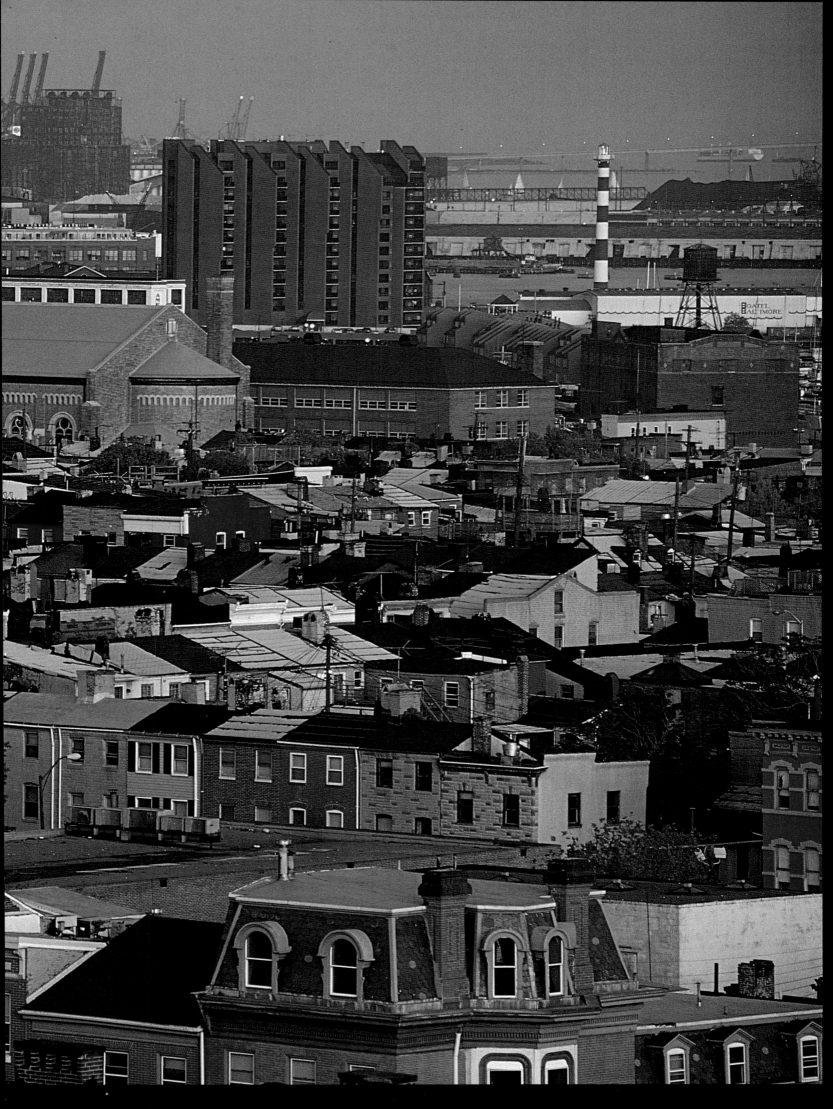

port, and industrial might — where a sprawl of row houses accommodated immigrants seeking a better life.

FOREWORD

SEARCHING FOR THE IMAGE

They've been searching for it for years: a single theme that would express Baltimore — the youngest of America's old cities.

It's either 192 or 262 (depending on whether you use its incorporation or its charter date as the birthday) but in either case there's been plenty of time to get things together into a national symbol. That's not the way Baltimore works, however. It's a succession of events, a melange of movements that accent variety.

The real question is how can a city define itself. It's a question as old as Athens and in photography I feel artists have found a superbly appropriate medium for defining twentieth century municipalities. The old and new Baltimore is the fiber of this book and the Evans lens reveals it as a place generally joyous, one that loves animals and crowds and sporting events — a place that vibrates with outdoor festivals, conventions and urban fairs, today virtually year-round events around the town.

Water gave the city life, the Chesapeake Bay in the main, but also upland geography and its forgotten contribution. The city was the last and southernmost of the east coast's major fall-line sieves, a place laced with tumbling creeks near tidewater. This meant innumerable mills along the Patapsco basin, working things that could get commerce going — corn, flour, and the product of cotton factories — as the city began to set world standards for grain products, sailcloth and "cotton duck."

Today, some of the mills are still there and the harbor that really gave birth to the city has been brilliantly focused as a national convention center after a transfusion of roughly $2 billion in new construction. An image was born. People could finally see the city in one sweeping and exhilirating cliche (ideally viewed from historic Federal Hill). Beyond the downtown's towers reflected in inner harbor waters lay the older city. The harbor may have had overtones of San Francisco or Singapore, but there was more — lots more.

Despite its white step and row house image, the fact is that Baltimore was something more than a one-note town architecturally. But outside of residential patterns, it never developed a uniform, stylistic feeling. Geography made things heterogeneous. There was never a chance (as originally planned) of following Philadelphia's flat grid of streets, because Baltimore was mostly hills. (If Rome was built on seven hills, Baltimore must be built on at least a hundred!) That ruled out standardization. The city simply created its arteries to fall where they could, largely, just to be streets where the poor could strive and the lucky prosper.

A uniform, stylistic feeling (despite all those white steps) seemed unachievable as an image. There was never a counterpart to the white towers of Miami, the Georgian gloss of Boston, the skyscraper verticality of Chicago or San Francisco's bay fronts. But there was variety here, far more than large-scale cities sometimes offer, especially out in middle America and along the sunbelt. With this variety went all sorts of malleable horizons that could be molded structurally and detailed in infinite ways. Things had to be adapted to sites that bubbled with hillsides and leaked with flood-prone waterways. The angularities, the infinite changes began at the harbor where the underlying rock layers are so ancient, they show no trace of organic remains, and the changes continue as you move farther from center city.

Above this layer, buildings and heights slope upward for about twenty miles and nearly a quarter of a mile in altitude. Pools of light shoot down into lowlands and creek and river valleys; highlands are saluted at dawn and sunset by the sun. In some spots, like sequestered Dickeyville, glades of Leakin park, the lower Jones Falls valley with its packed accretion of ancient mill buildings, old Frederick road and the slopes of Oella above the Patapsco, it's a shadowy, cool world that doesn't seem to focus with a roaring metro area at all.

Photography, it seems to me, is the ideal medium for expressing urban images, with its patient all inclusiveness, far beyond the evanescent nature of TV and film, hurrying on, all too often just to titillate. It grants time, allowing the mind to roam free at will, without imposing narrative or ongoing change upon you. Perhaps there are things, of course, that photos cannot express, like the grand emotional fortitudes of the likes of Shakespeare, Beethoven or Michelangelo or the inner spirit of faith and mysticism. But what it says is uniquely adapted to an America with all its practicalities and follies.

In this regard, the Baltimore climate cooperates beautifully. It is, by turns, unique, blustery, radiant and dreary, a thing rightly mourned over the years as a thing of endless change. The singular quality is so cooperative. Whatever mood you wish to create with a lens — drizzle, dazzle or something in between, it will produce as sure as God gave western Maryland little green apples.

Most images are by nature things of the present. But you cannot frame a thought about the city without the past, too, being somehow near if you probe a bit. This is a city that kept quiet about its assets for so long that they were forgotten almost as if part of a foreign country. Yet the Walters Art Gallery, save for Boston's similar Gardner collection, is one of the western world's only remaining nineteenth century comprehensive art collections, conceived by one family and left, miraculously intact, as a testimony to culture. Of equal rank, and wholly complementary, is the Baltimore Museum of Art, with world class strengths in late Renaissance works, textiles, prints, impressionist and post-impressionist artists and the abstract art.

Probably, in proportion to its size, no American city owes as much to single philanthropists as Baltimore. The hospital and university of Johns Hopkins, the institute and conservatory of George Peabody, and the mental health center of Moses Sheppard and Enoch Pratt are world-renowned. More recent endowments have included a $40 million fund raised for the Baltimore Symphony Orchestra, now a world tour attraction. The symphony is one of America's few that is housed in a hall it owns, thanks to the generosity of the Joseph Meyerhoff family.

The fact is that the city boasts more than a few attractions that outdate the nineteenth and twentieth century creations. Among them are the city markets, serving such city nodes as Union Square, Highlandtown, Upton and Oldtown and above all the near west side. The markets, especially the enormous Lexington street affair (dating from 1751, believe it or not!) are survivals of a type that are disappearing even in large European cities. They remain a colorful link with the city's short, 45-year Colonial history before the Revolution. Every century since it was founded, in fact, has added lustre to the local and national culture. The eminent Maryland Historical Society and the Maryland Academy of Sciences were both founded before the Civil War and so was the medical faculty of the University of Maryland. All three exhibit a vibrant present and a vibrant past of 150 years or more.

Modern central Baltimore is an outdoor museum of early and late twentieth century architectural styles. This is partly a function of the building boom that resulted after the entire downtown center burned in February 1904. The boom provided so much office space that almost no new buildings were needed until the end of the 1950s. Beginning with the Charles Center redevelopment project, and with the building of the Blaustein tower and One Charles Center, the north end of the harbor sprouted dramatic buildings that contrasted with earlier masonry and formed a dramatic curtain behind the 195-year-old U.S.F. *Constellation* and ships of call from world ports that find the inner harbor's bulkheading irresistible. Main players in the inner harbor visual drama include an IBM company addition with a tower structure that recalls the shape of sails, the waterside World Trade Center, The National Aquarium, seven hotels, a towering condo and the home office of the United States Fidelity & Guaranty Company. The last named created an amusing spectator "what is it" while building progressed. A stalk-thin concrete structure only 17 feet wide but 500 feet high crept skyward. Natural parallax of the eye made the thin core structure seem to bend to many people. "It's crooked," were some of the sidewalk super-intendent comments, an impression corrected when the building was finished.

The average Baltimore citizen seems quietly proud that twenty years of effort has given his home city a spectacular downtown with anchored structures like a new stadium for his beloved Orioles baseball club. Somehow the huge, dramatic new structure doesn't overwhelm or stamp out the memory of sports of long ago, so intimately told in the Babe Ruth baseball museum, only paces away from the new major league park.

Is it north, or is it south, is often asked of Baltimore, a question that in a way defines the dilemma of character that faces its citizens. In the deep south or the windy west it would never occur to citizens to worry about their orientation. But in some ways, the Baltimorean does and debates are even held that question whether the city (and the state) were loyal in the Civil War or were more attached to the destiny of Dixie and the Bonnie Blue Flag.

Of course it doesn't matter, but it lies under the curiously unselfconscious character of many local citizens, often a man who literally doesn't give a damn what people think about him in Louisville or Kalamazoo.

As a creature of the late twentieth century, however, local citizens have their identifiable "ways." There's that accent called Baltimorese, that surviving lingo spoken by many hundreds of thousands of older east and west side natives and their descendants in the city and the five surrounding counties. Mainly it involves giving an extra, non-existent syllable to some words, like "cynic" for sink and "muriel" for mural. There's also a habit of giving a rolling "o" sound to vowels that don't deserve it. (The language is supposed to be a blend of Philadelphiese and Dixie talk, but somehow this description misses the mark.) No matter what their calling, all the folk are supposed to be from Balamer or even more currently Balmer. This is uniform throughout true natives who prefer it over other alternatives, like the Balmow you can hear south of the Rappahanock river in Virginia and points south or the Bal-tee-more that you can hear in England, Boston and other "correct" latitudes.

One thing all Baltimore shares is an epidemic and rather unreasonable fear of snow. A two or three-inch snow shower that wouldn't make the nightly news in Pittsburgh and in Buffalo would go completely unnoticed, sets off a multi-media driver's panic involving at least a quarter of a million autos, creeping through the evening rush hour. Nobody seems to notice that on many roads, despite rashes of fender benders, the snowstorm crawl is actually safer than everyday travel in good weather when everybody is fast-laning at 67 mph.

Beyond these foibles, there's a sort of conscious air of "make-do" in the Baltimore character. People do not live by poses, indeed, the citizen doesn't seem to think of himself as a special person or privileged dude unless he is doing something like attending a World Series game, a Preakness race or a big time rock concert. Casualness is the norm. That is why the work of local photographers is likely to catch informality, naturalness on the wing, a refreshing change in a world saturated with staged media poses and artificial or rehearsed action. A Baltimorean knows the difference.

To view the center city today, one would never know that in the 1960s civic morale reached the lowest point since the 1860s when, for more than four years, the city was constricted with military rule during the great conflict of the Civil War. Since the tragic 1960s the metro area has literally found itself, or perhaps refound itself. It is a place of parades and patriots unabashed, with the third largest American Legion post in the world. It is a place to go to get well. It is a place you go to find out if cities really still work, not the only place by far for such a judgment, but one that shares the country's biggest challenge — finding out whether municipal man is to be tamed and the killing is to stop.

There it is, a city of flags. A parade of time. A place that housed and homed in some fashion every single emigrant race that came its way, even the Lumbee Indian tribes of North Carolina origin. It has been a nursery of pride and an employment lab. Not the least of its honors is the fact that it is a place that 150 years ago housed 30,000 free blacks (they outnumbered local slaves ten to one), possibly the largest and best schooled urban African community in the world, thanks to the heroic efforts of black churches and Afro-American teachers. Black workers included thousands of mechanics and laborers who worked to finance the church schools, who caulked ten thousand boats for half a century and hauled the billion-bricked city into being. It was a place that soaked up immigrant brain power like some urban sponge — Greek, German, Italian, Polish, Latvian, Irish, French and scores of other origins, men and women who built and worked 4,000 industries into being. It's a place that has created music and art foundations that rival European communities and it has fostered scientific study and most especially medical advances beyond calculation.

It can be lonely to be all that and be unknown, which is why many Baltimoreans are confronted with blank stares in other locales they visit. To get the temper of town you must look down the city's alleys that are fading away or half vacant with decay or being scrubbed up and gentrified for the new tenantry. Here walked the dark spirits of Edgar Allan Poe and John Wilkes Booth and here music presses clacked away through the night, printing the sad songs of Stephen Collins Foster as the pianos tinkled in the big row house parlors and men in caped coats signed into Barnum's hotel while the julep bar tinkled across the street at Guy's Monument house and echoed with the murmer of men.

That is Baltimore's muted and masculine romance — a doer's place that puts out multiple images, kaleidoscopes of a half-forgotten past and a future far away.

— Carleton Jones

No smiles on the faces of these parade-goers. A young spectator **(left)** at the I Am An American Day Parade is anxious for the patriotic procession to begin. A brief shower during the Shriners Parade **(above)** dampens the spirits of the Boumi Temple clowns, but not for long. At the Columbus Day Parade, a child of Peruvian ancestry **(below)** is overwhelmed by the commotion.

INTRODUCTION

When people ask me what I do for a living, I sometimes reply that I am a "professional tourist." On one of my more glamorous assignments, I met up with the *Pride of Baltimore II* in London for a journey to Weymouth on England's southern coast. As she passed beneath the Tower Bridge during a day sail on the Thames, an English photographer who was shooting next to me on the embankment asked, "What a beauty; do you know where she hails from?" — to which I gladly replied, "my hometown, Baltimore." Yet his inquiry elicited more than a series of words, as a warm feeling from within carved a big smile on my face. These days, being a Baltimorean is something to feel good about, and this change of heart is what I have been exploring for the past several years.

On comparing unflattering slogans of Baltimore past — "Mobtown," for example — with those of late — "Charm City," "Renaissance City," and "Baltimore is Best"—it is evident that a new era has dawned over this realm. In the following pages, I hope to shed some light on the transformation that has unfolded within the span of my lifetime. Beyond documenting our quality of life, which has improved for a large segment of the population, I hope also to surprise and educate on the vast Baltimore mosaic — a wealth of special attractions, traditions, peoples, and institutions of consequence.

As an informed citizen, I am well aware of the multitude of urban ills that afflict our city, and I do not mean to downplay their gravity, but I will leave it up to the media to address these issues. This book is offered as a celebration of the revitalization of an aging industrial sprawl into a thriving American metropolis. That is not to say that a cantankerous old lady has been metamorphasized into a sophisticated beauty who cherishes life and embraces all who cross her path. Nagging problems persist despite the sincere efforts of the city fathers who are expected to solve them; and the well-documented charm of contemporary Baltimore owes much to her glorious past: a strong ethnic and maritime heritage, a colorful history, an embracement of neighborhood identity, and the crafting of architectural and institutional gems. This solid foundation has served as a sturdy backbone during Baltimore's reemergence, and so it will in this book. On considering the bleak outlook of the city just a few decades ago, it is quite an accomplishment that Baltimore has summoned the energy not merely to march, but to stride toward a bright future, when so many cities are still lumbering in the shadows of despair.

*   *   *   *

It pleases me greatly that distinguished journalist Carleton Jones, a resident of Maryland since 1952, has agreed to share his time-honored perspective on Baltimore past and present. Retired in 1992 from the *Baltimore Sun*, Jones was a features writer for a quarter century, covering a range of topics, from general news and Baltimore folklore, to restaurants, real estate, and personalities. On his favorite topic, Maryland historical lore, Jones has written four books; the most recent, *Streetwise Baltimore*, explores the sometimes peculiar nomenclature and anecdotes relating to scores of local streets. In addition, he has led adult education tours in and around Baltimore, sponsored by the Johns Hopkins University and the Smithsonian Institution.

On the completion of my first book, *Maryland In Focus* — a photographic documentary of the bountiful "Land of Pleasant Living," published in November 1988 — I realized that I had only scratched the surface of Baltimore. Captivated by my hometown, my next project was clear; the only questions concerned how to best accomplish the task. Decisions had to be made on the tactics and parameters which would guide me through a hectic three years allotted to record Baltimore life. And to that end, I would like to share some of the frustrations and triumphs encountered along the way.

While journeying through this photographic kaleidoscope, the reader will see that my inquiring eyes were not confined within the Baltimore city line. Initially, I planned to document only the city proper, but the overwhelming sense of community that I soon discovered seemed to transcend the divisions created by political boundaries. Interaction between the city and its environs, facilitated by the accessibility of the downtown district, has become so entrenched in the lifestyle of its citizens, that excluding the surrounding area would be comparable to displaying a grand old painting without a frame. As Central Maryland constitutes a significant expanse of territory, I decided that a ten-mile band (give or take) around the city seemed to be a reasonable limit. Thus, when referring to "Baltimore," I am also speaking of this annexation.

Concerning the range of subject matter to photograph, I placed no restrictions on myself. Confronted with a dazzling array of things to do and see, I felt compelled to present Baltimore from a variety of viewpoints. Hence, a broad spectrum of topics is offered: the arts, history, architecture, the economy, nightlife, sports, nature, special events and attractions. As the scope of the book broadens, of course, the ability to thoroughly cover a particular theme narrows. It would not be practical to include all of the institutions, events, and cultural expressions that deserve recognition. Nonetheless, I realize that this volume, when compared to other "coffeetable" photography books, is substantial. I offer this collection not only to support my claim that variety is standout among Baltimore's famed attractions, but to explore the potency of photography as a medium for artistic expression. As an avid collector of photographic documentaries, I have developed a preference for books that cannot be fully digested in one viewing and then sentenced to an early retirement on the bookshelf. I hope that this volume continues to provide enjoyment every time it is paged.

*   *   *   *

I have employed a reliable strategy in assembling this collection of nearly 300 photographs. What I look for in a photograph is an interesting subject, a revealing moment in the life of that subject, and a pleasing composition which integrates the subject and background elements. Sometimes it is best to isolate the subject with a uniform, non-distracting background; other times it is more interesting to depict the subject in its environment. The initial step in this sometimes lengthy process is also the most crucial — generating an idea for subject matter. Inspiration can have a variety of sources. As a native Baltimorean, a logical starting point was to review personal life experiences.

My earliest and most cherished memories involve exploring areas close to home with my family. Two favorite playgrounds were, and continue to be, Sherwood Gardens, a paradise of pastels where flocks of spring fever victims seek relief, and Lake Roland, a suburban frontier where miniature lobsters can be plucked from the rocky stream below the towering waterfalls. For a taste of history our family ventured to the home of a massive and most celebrated flag, Fort

McHenry, and to a magical assemblage of trains, the B&O Railroad Museum. En route to Fort McHenry, we passed the Inner Harbor, but there was no reason then, in 1975, to stop there — simply because there was nothing to see. Driving through the city sometimes provided glimpses of local curiosities: arabs, or "gypsies" as I called them then, parading their pony-powered wagons, overflowing with produce, and paintings of pastoral scenes on the screen doors of row houses in neighborhoods where countless rows of white marble steps raced towards the horizon. I also recall visiting my grandfather at the magnificent mansion called Evergreen, where he volunteered in his later years as a caretaker of its treasured book and coin collections. Ironically, as an enthusiastic book collector, he amassed one of the finest libraries of Maryland lore, yet he suffered from a disabling illness which became acute just as I was developing this common interest . . . and he passed away just months before I would be able to add my own work to his collection.

No cultural indoctrination of the Baltimore lifestyle would be complete without lessons in the dissection of the unsightly, but ever-so-tasty blue crab, and an introduction to the "fastest game on foot" — lacrosse. At an early age I had delusions of glory playing at Homewood Field, but unfortunately this was not to be. I have attended many Hopkins games where, in addition to a fine Blue Jay performance, I have enjoyed mixing with the crowd and seeing friends. As Marylanders are also known to enjoy the water, I looked forward to fishing excursions aboard the *Osprey*, our family powerboat, which was not as adept in finding fish as its namesake. Fortunately, we had no problem tracking the majestic tall ships as they sailed up the Chesapeake Bay and Patapsco River during the bicentennial summer of 1976.

Another rite of summer was cheering on the Orioles, glove in hand, at Memorial Stadium. It is ironic how, as a child, I remember hoping desperately (and in vain) that the arc of a foul ball would intersect my outstretched arm, but as a professional photographer on the sidelines, I have barely escaped several errant rockets which could shatter a lens or bruise a body. Of all the great moments I witnessed at Memorial Stadium, including action-packed Baltimore Colts' games, photographing President Bush throwing out the first pitch on Opening Day in 1989 outranks them all. Jockeying for position among dozens of eager photographers trying to avoid the obstructed views cast by an army of secret service agents, I realized that I was playing in the major leagues, and on that occasion, I scored a victory. Also carved into my memory is the last baseball game at Memorial Stadium, concluded by a delightful yet haunting ceremony when scores of Oriole greats took to the field for a final curtain call, accompanied by the "Field of Dreams" theme song. Ripples of shivers rolled across my skin as a lifetime of memories struggled hopelessly to reach an inner equilibrium. It is often said that baseball in Baltimore takes on a special meaning, and for those who witnessed this final farewell, that truth is crystal clear.

With joy I have incorporated these bits and pieces from my past, but I also recognize the limitations associated with one person's heritage. Out of respect to the responsibilities of journalism, I have attempted to educate myself on the common experiences of fellow Baltimoreans. A most productive source has been the media; scanning newspapers, magazines, and books have also proved fruitful. Other useful tips were provided by television and radio programs. I have welcomed suggestions from friends and the scores of interested people that this project has afforded me the opportunity to meet. A final plan of attack is to simply get lost with the hope of stumbling upon something special.

Once a subject seems promising, I then consider under what conditions will there be a defining moment worth preserving. Such determining factors include season, time of day, weather, lighting, angle of view, and the potential to incorporate contributing elements into the composition. Beyond these particulars, some public relations is also necessary, especially in dealing with institutions. The majority of my requests were well received, and a few required persistence, but only one was repeatedly denied.

The final stage in this process is to execute the photograph. It is also frustrating because I have little or no control over the variables which create the special, sometimes magical moment. From experience I have learned that such instants are elusive, and are captured only after relentless pursuit. A classic example is the shot of a colorful windsurfing race. During the first of three summers that I worked on this book, I attended several regattas sponsored by the Baltimore Area Boardsailing Association. Needless to say, a key variable is wind, which is especially fickle during the summer; on each of these highly anticipated race days Mother Nature delivered a Baltimore summertime sizzler — a muggy, windless steam bath. After hours of waiting, only a slight breeze whispered by, as if to say "better luck next time." The following summer, my luck had not improved, yet I had one last chance. A September regatta was scheduled; the day was unusually calm, as three or four restless hours passed, and participants were starting to pack up their rigs. Just in the nick of time a gentle breeze evolved into a wind, and two exciting races were squeezed in before a ferocious thunderstorm hit. At last.

Fortunately, only about a dozen such projects were so excruciating. Nonetheless, each photograph in this collection required an average of three or four outings to capture the moment. My essential challenge has been to anticipate and witness telling moments in the life of Baltimore. Once a tolerance is developed for all the necessary scouting trips, public relations, driving, backaches from hauling equipment, waiting, and retakes, the mechanics of recording them on film is a relatively painless task.

*   *   *   *

While enjoying wonderful photo opportunities since embarking on this hometown rediscovery, my curiosity has been rewarded with a firsthand education in the special institutions, peoples, and landmarks that distinguish our community. Some places command a high profile, and I was eager to learn more. Two such institutions which have brought international attention to Baltimore are the R Adams Cowley Shock Trauma Center at University Hospital and the Johns Hopkins Hospital. I was privileged to gain access to Shock Trauma's helipad and admitting area, where victims receive immediate care on arrival. The suffering was unpleasant to see, but I was overpowered by the drama of doctors and nurses rising to the challenge of repairing bodies afflicted with life-threatening injury. The aggregate brainpower and technology was quite humbling. A second impressive facility that I visited, this time within the medical maze of the Johns Hopkins Hospital, was the neonatal intensive care unit, where premature babies — sometimes weighing only a pound at birth — are nursed back to health. I was amazed to learn that many of these fragile lives recover fully from such precarious entries into the world.

On the spiritual side of life, the Bethel African Methodist Episcopal Church, also a leader in its field, has made a strong impression on me. On entering the church to photograph a service, I was made to feel welcome as a stranger. The service commenced with a communal prayer during which the congregation held hands. My neighbors on either side reached out to me without hesitation, laying to rest my initial sense of uneasiness. Worship within this pillar of the black community was freely expressed with such passion that I had no doubt as to the congregation's religious convictions.

My explorations have also taken me to places which escape the limelight, but on investigation, have proven to be intriguing. En route to various destinations, I have stumbled across many of Baltimore's unique neighborhoods, and one of the most pleasant surprises was Dickeyville. After navigating through a depressed section of West Baltimore, I suddenly found myself on Wetherdsville Road, which meanders along the lush Gwynns Falls valley — so lush and remote, it seemed, that it had no business being in a city — until a scaled-down Shangri-la appeared. It doesn't take much imagination to picture Beaver Cleaver whizzing by on a scooter, waving to the mailman in this once-prosperous mill town, suspended in time.

Speaking of places resistant to change, Baltimore has a number of striking cemeteries. Of particular interest is Green Mount, enclosed by imposing stone walls and a fanciful gatehouse. Many times I had driven past without giving a thought as to what lay within. One day I finally drove in and explored with amazement this labyrinth of crypts, headstones, and monuments, clustered over the peaks and valleys of Green Mount's manicured terrain. There is a distinct aura about the place, though it took several trips over different seasons to pin it down in a photograph.

An experience that will be savored for a lifetime is sailing aboard our seafaring ambassador, the *Pride of Baltimore II*. While preparing for *Maryland In Focus*, I had hoped for such an opportunity aboard the *Pride of Baltimore*, but that hope vanished when she was claimed by a freak storm off the coast of Puerto Rico in 1986. Nonetheless, the same kind of energy which has rejuvenated our city was channelled into the building of a new clipper ship, the *Pride of Baltimore II*, launched in the spring of 1988. When work on this book commenced the following winter, the *Pride II* topped my assignment list. My request was warmly received, and after a year of sorting out details, final arrangements were made to sail with the ship from Venezuela to Puerto Rico.

Our sail across the Caribbean was unusually smooth. The weather was terrific, and everyone was in good spirits. The highlight of the trip was a mid-sea swim, which doubled as a long-awaited bath for most of us. Diving from various perches into the warm, crystal clear turquoise water was sheer jubilation, a fleeting return to the innocence of childhood. There were, however, two tense moments which served as humbling reminders of the perils of sailing on a class of ship designed at the turn of the eighteenth century. First, embarking from Caracas late one evening, the port side of the ship accidently brushed against pilings alongside the dock; the added tension on the rigging caused the main topmast to snap in two. Debris fell to the deck as a 20-foot portion of the topmast dangled precariously about our heads. Several of the more experienced sailors scrambled high into the darkness, and after an hour of careful maneuvering and rope work, they

managed to secure the heavy spar, until it could be lowered to the deck for repair. The feat was nothing short of spectacular, at least from the perspective of a landlubber. The second perilous moment occurred some three days later when I was photographing sailors on the bowsprit. Supported by a single rope beneath my feet, I suddenly encountered the biggest wave of the trip. The skyward rise of the crest of the wave was exhilarating, but the subsequent plunge bordered on terrifying. The rapid fall culminated in a good dunking for me. Luckily, I did not lose my footing, and the only casualty (beside by ego) was one of my cameras, which slammed into the bowsprit.

My most lucid memory, however, was a happy one. Navigating one glorious Caribbean evening at the helm by one of a myriad of visible stars, a gentle breeze, neither warm nor cool, rolled over my skin, giving me a soothing sensation of complete peace. All of the challenges and stresses of life were as distant as the nearest shoreline, hidden from view by the curvature of earth.

*   *   *   *

One of the most consuming interests in my life besides photography is wildlife; fortunately the two go hand-in-hand. I have never outgrown a childhood fascination with animals. On the contrary, it has grown stronger, especially on discovering that the local environment teems with many kinds of creatures. Since most of our native species go about their business unnoticed to the untrained eye, it is exciting to discover just what is out there. Though most local populations are faring pretty well, I am alarmed at the plight of wildlife across the globe. Moreover, I am convinced that photographers can address this dilemma by capturing the attention of the public with striking, informative pictures, and I have begun to nurture this conviction.

A particularly keen interest of mine is birds, an affection explained partly because our feathered friends are more visible and thus easier to photograph than other forms of wildlife, and partly because they are so diverse in size, shape, color, and behavior. The variety of bird life in Maryland is staggering; there are hundreds of perennial and migrant species, featuring such characters as the red-bellied woodpecker and the black-crowned night-heron. One way to observe birds up close is to give them what they want: food. A good example is my effort in luring into camera range the stunning American goldfinch — the adult male is bright yellow with a black cap and wings. I purchased the recommended feeder and thistle seeds; within days these winged jewels were refueling on a regular basis. Another highlight of my avian experiences was documenting nesting peregrine falcons in downtown Baltimore. Photographing wild birds normally involves building a blind in some remote place and enduring the elements for hours on end, as I did to capture nesting herons and egrets within a protected harbor oasis. Yet in the case of this dynamic species, which has adapted to civilization in unusual ways, all one has to do (with permission, of course) is take an elevator to the 33rd floor of the USF&G building and peer through a conference room window onto their cliff-like nest.

A favorite place to come close to nature is the Baltimore Zoo, where I have whiled away many an afternoon. The zoo that I remember as a child is very different from the zoo of today, which has vastly improved the quality of the habitats. The trend away from bars and concrete toward natural spaces with unobstructed views has created marvelous opportunities for the photographer. The major requirement for special shots is a willingness to wait for the right moment, whether it be a telling pose, unusual behavior, or facial expression. I made a point of visiting the new polar bears within days of their introduction, when they were especially frisky. For the hour that I watched them play, I was a child again, delighted by their aquatic wrestling bouts and dispute over ownership of a floating ball.

Another spectacular showcase for nature's bounty is the National Aquarium, where one finds a dazzling array of fish, sporting colors to rival any palette, as well as marine amphibians, reptiles, mammals, and birds. Photography inside this architectural curiosity offers new challenges since most subjects are behind glass in soft lighting, necessitating a flash. I discovered that lighting through glass is very tricky, and it took a good deal of trial and error to work out the bugs during nearly twenty trips I made over two winters. Fortunately, the Aquarium makes an inviting classroom, and the tedium of on-the-job training was offset by a fascination with the plethora of life swimming, flying, and slithering around me. I was especially anxious about the opening of the Marine Mammal Pavilion; the impressive demonstration of the intelligence and acrobatics of its dolphins and beluga whales lived up to my high expectations. What surprised me was their apparent enthusiasm for performing, as if these distant relatives from the sea could not only detect the appreciation of their audience, but reveled in it.

Special recognition is due a particular animal, known not only for its power and beauty, but for all of the economic, sporting, and social activity that it generates. As the delicious blue crab is an adopted symbol of the state, so the graceful horse is an equally appropriate emblem for Central Maryland, symbolizing a society and way of life deeply rooted in the gentle landscape of its counties. When thinking of horses, the Preakness and the Maryland Hunt Cup instantly come to mind. For most interested Baltimoreans, these two racing events are all that they might experience of our rich equestrian heritage. Yet for the inveterate outdoorsman, there is much more to see. The sport that provided the biggest surprise of my journeys through horse country was polo, which I more readily associated with far away places like Florida and England than with Timonium and Monkton, where the Maryland Polo Club steps into high gear. What I discovered was an intense contact sport mixing precision timing, motion, and communication between man and animal — in other words, the kind of sport that yields only a few knockout photographs, if any, for a day's work.

*   *   *   *

In preparing this collection, I have confronted an assortment of obstacles, setbacks, and frustrations, spread over some 200 assignments. Periodically the tension has mounted to the brink of sheer exasperation, and I wanted to call it quits, but I knew that I could not. Two powerful motivating forces have kept me going, beyond the fundamental need to earn a living. First, I have developed a passion for the craft of photography over the six years that it has been my profession. The photograph is a potent tool for communication; the message can be absorbed within the blink of an eye. An occasional image is so powerful that it shoots through the eyes and pounds on the heart. Enjoying the effect, the challenge of

causing it has become the driving force of my life. One aspect of photography which I find so enticing is the variety of challenges it poses. Whereas some professionals carve their market niche in a specific area — nature, sports, portraiture, or medicine, for example — I like to play the role of maverick photographer, wetting my feet in a variety of arenas. All this aside, the essential lure of photography is the magic of being able to create a tangible record of any sight that the world has to offer, to share the prize with others or simply hang it on a wall; and, in doing so, somehow allay the stark reality of one's own mortality.

A second, equally compelling source of inspiration is a growing sense of pride in being a Baltimorean. In comparing the Baltimore of my childhood with the Baltimore of today, I am amazed at the transformation. The face of the city has an entirely new look; older buildings have been razed while new structures shoot up like spring flowers, creating an impressive skyline. At the core of this renaissance is the Inner Harbor, a dynamic year-round entertainment mecca luring visitors from afar. Only two decades ago this stretch of waterfront was virtually devoid of commerce and culture. As of late, Baltimoreans can also boast of Oriole Park at Camden Yards, hailed by the media as one of America's finest ballparks. I was among the fortunate who attended the first regular season game on April 6, 1992. What a show was Opening Day! Even after a decade of unprecedented change, the renaissance has yet to abate. What will the next ten years bring?

Yet behind the scenes of revitalization, Baltimore persists with a small-town feel, delighting with pleasures and traditions from an era not too long ago, when her reputation was not so favorable. Clearly, she has cast a spell on her people, for so many with Baltimore roots, though sometimes tempted away for a time, choose to return and settle here. Whatever the reason, few can deny being touched by the wave of pride that carries our city forward. I offer these pictures not just to stimulate the senses, but to recognize and salute all of the people who are part of the Baltimore success story.

Middleton Evans
June 3, 1992

Above: *A fireboat of the Baltimore City Fire Department spouts off a tall welcome to a visiting tall ship. Overlooking the Inner Harbor is the Legg Mason Tower, completed in 1988 as the new headquarters of Legg Mason, a leading regional investment firm founded in Baltimore. The distinctive complex also includes the Stouffer Hotel and a shopping mall.*

Left: *Once the pinnacle of grandeur on the Baltimore skyline, the white dome of City Hall is now overshadowed by the Signet Tower and a host of other office buildings. Due to costly maintenance problems, this relic from the post-Civil War era was scheduled to be razed in 1975, but preservationists came to the rescue and City Hall has been completely restored.*

Preceding pages: *Treasures along Baltimore's waterfront, such as the U.S. Coast Guard cutter Roger B. Taney (a survivor of the Japanese attack on Pearl Harbor in 1941), testify to a city deeply rooted in maritime tradition.*

Magnificent buildings crown the Homewood campus of the Johns Hopkins University, including Gilman Hall **(left)**, which contains the undergraduate Hutzler Reading Room **(below)**, and Homewood **(above)**, a Federal period museum house. Founded in 1876 as the nation's first true university — a graduate institution where scholarship is pursued within a research environment — Johns Hopkins arose from the philanthropy of its namesake, a shrewd Baltimore merchant and financier who bequeathed $7 million in 1873 for its establishment along with a hospital. Now the country's leading research university, based on the value of private and government contracts, Johns Hopkins is comprised of seven academic divisions. At the heart of this network is the 140-acre Homewood campus in North Baltimore, home to the schools of Arts and Sciences and Engineering.

Above: *Quaint homes and white picket fences make Dickeyville one of Baltimore's most charming neighborhoods. Sheltered by a wooded stream valley along the city's western fringe, Dickeyville dates back to 1762, when the first mill was erected along the Gwynns Falls. The thriving mill town that enveloped its banks produced goods well into this century, but as its industrial heyday waned, Dickeyville entered its second era of prosperity as a prime residential community.*

Left: *West Baltimore from the air reveals colorful clusters of row houses. Many of Baltimore's nearly 250 neighborhoods take on such a uniform appearance, but in character they show remarkable diversity.*

Beautiful houses of worship are vivid testimony to the strength of the Roman Catholic Church in Baltimore, selected in 1789 as the nation's first diocese. The massive Cathedral of Mary Our Queen **(above)** was opened in 1959 as the archdiocese's second cathedral. This contemporary Gothic church, noted for its imposing twin towers and inspiring decorations, serves a large parish of 4,000 in North Baltimore. St. Leo the Great Roman Catholic Church **(below)** is one of the most picturesque neighborhood churches, erected in Little Italy in 1881 for the growing community of Italian immigrants. The most celebrated landmark of the city's robust Catholic legacy is the Basilica of the Assumption **(right)**, completed in 1821 as the country's first metropolitan cathedral. The magnificent nave ranks high on the list of America's most distinguished interiors.

Left and below: *Baltimore/Washington International Airport is Maryland's only major international airport, operated by the State Aviation Administration in north Anne Arundel County, just ten miles from downtown Baltimore. KLM Royal Dutch Airlines, which began BWI's first non-stop service to the continent of Europe in 1990, is one of twenty-three commercial airlines serving BWI; on an average day some 28,000 passengers and 675 flights move through the airport.*

Right: *Elevated highways keep the traffic moving over wetlands of the Middle Branch of the Patapsco River. Among major East Coast cities, metropolitan Baltimore offers perhaps the finest transportation infrastructure, including six interstate highways, ample warehouse space, a host of modern marine facilities at the port, and some 600 miles of railroad track.*

Above: *A cozy Victorian porch typifies Roland Park, one of Baltimore's most beautiful neighborhoods. Established in 1891, great pride is taken in its distinction as one of the country's first planned communities. Situated on a sloping ridge overlooking the Jones Falls in North Baltimore, the garden suburb of Roland Park is noted for its rugged topography, where gracious homes of various architectural styles, winding roads, and meandering footpaths blend in with the natural vegetation and lofty trees.*

Left: *Cloaked in a white blanket, Pastel Row serves as a colorful nucleus of Charles Village, a popular North Baltimore community where urban renewal has transformed the neighborhood. Beginning in the 1950s, many of its elegant turn-of-the-century townhouses have been reclaimed by an influx of new homeowners who have learned about renovation the hard way, often investing years of labor to restore the grandeur of their spacious homes. In 1967 the name Charles Village was chosen as part of an organized campaign to forge a new neighborhood identity.*

Above: A favorite room of the Enoch Pratt Free Library is the Maryland Department, decorated with murals depicting scenes from Spencer's "Faerie Queen." The Pratt is one of the country's most extensive municipal library systems, with twenty-eight branch libraries in "The City That Reads." The library's benefactor, Enoch Pratt — a transplanted Yankee who made his fortune in Baltimore — decided that Baltimore was in need of a public library, and he was willing to allocate a portion of his wealth to make that possible, providing that the city would establish a perpetual annuity for its upkeep.

Below and left: Since its founding in 1857 by George Peabody, the Peabody Institute has enriched the cultural life of Baltimore. Originally conceived in four parts, a conservatory and preparatory now comprise the Peabody, which was affiliated with the Johns Hopkins University in 1977. The Conservatory of Music — the nation's first professional music school — educates nearly 500 gifted young musicians from across the country and the world, representing more than twenty nations. The striking geometry of the George Peabody Library **(left)** — also a division of Johns Hopkins University — makes it one of America's finest library rooms, noted for its five tiers of ornate cast-iron balconies.

The tugboat America answers the call to duty at North Locust Point, where a departing bulk cargo ship dwarfs a

sailboat; traffic jams are common on the Patapsco River, gateway to Baltimore for over three centuries.

Above and left: *Colorful sailboats incite spring fever during the Chesapeake Bay Boat Show, held each winter at the Baltimore Convention Center. This gem of modern architecture is located just one block west of the Inner Harbor, featuring over 150,000 square feet of exhibit space. Festival Hall was added in 1985 to host public shows and community events. Proposals have been submitted to double the capacity of the Baltimore Convention Center so that larger events can be accommodated. Outside of the Convention Center visitors encounter a life-size sculpture of an artist at work. The handsome building in the background is 250 West Pratt Street.*

Right: *The downtown headquarters of Alex. Brown & Sons radiate the elegance of a bygone architectural era with decorative plaster molding, rich marble, and a spectacular Tiffany dome. This two-story brick fortress to America's senior investment banking house (founded in 1800) is also distinguished as one of the few survivors of the Great Fire of 1904, due to the absence of wood in its construction. By the time changing winds drove the fire to the harbor, virtually all of the business district had been wiped out.*

Following pages: *Different views show the ever-changing skyline of Baltimore.*

Above: *An arabber hooks up a pony at the Allen stable in Sandtown. This colorful tradition, well over a century old, turns commerce into a local art form, as the wagons and harnesses are highly ornamental. The few remaining arabbers travel established routes in the neighborhoods, providing seafood and produce to steady customers.*

Below: *The catch of the day awaits customers of Faidley's Seafood, a fifth-generation family business offering an astonishing 200 varieties of fresh seafood at its Lexington Market stall. Proclaiming itself the oldest continuously operated market in America, Lexington Market has faithfully served Baltimoreans since 1782.*

Right: *MTA buses and a new train of the Central Light Rail Line provide ample public transportation on Howard Street, once a beehive of Baltimore retailing. Operated by the Mass Transit Administration, light rail commenced operations in April 1992; the first line, upon completion, will run 22.5 miles between Timonium in Baltimore County and Glen Burnie in Anne Arundel County, with twenty-four stops.*

Above: *Angels hover over St. Michael as he slays the dragon on a brilliant stained-glass panel at St. Paul's Protestant Episcopal Church, whose parish was established in 1729. The present building of the "Mother Church of Baltimore" is styled as an Italian Romanesque basilica, the fourth church to occupy the site in downtown Baltimore. Among the church's beautiful stained-glass windows are several by Louis Comfort Tiffany.*

Right: *St. Michael's Ukranian Catholic Church is one of the most unusual additions to the mixture of Baltimore architecture, located across from Patterson Park in East Baltimore. The crowning glory of the old-style Ukranian church are its five onion-shaped domes, plated with copper and crested by gilded crosses. The three-year construction project — completed in 1991 at a cost of $3 million — realized a dream of St. Michael's parish first sparked more than a quarter-century ago.*

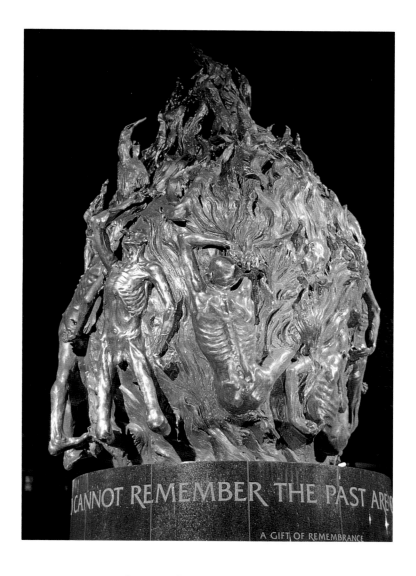

With more than 100 monuments decorating the urban landscape, it is little wonder that Baltimore is sometimes called the "Monumental City." Grand dame of local memorials, the 178-foot Washington Monument **(left)** was begun in 1815 as the nation's first to honor a most admirable president, yet it was built on a vacant hilltop overlooking the city for fear that the heavy column might fall over and crush unlucky admirers. The Lee-Jackson Monument **(above right)**, located in Wyman Park, shows Robert E. Lee and Stonewall Jackson of the Confederacy conferring before a battle; it is one of a few double-equestrian statues in existence. At the Holocaust Memorial just north of the Inner Harbor, a 14-foot bronze sculpture **(above left)**, dedicated in 1988, depicts the Holocaust victims in horrific detail; circumscribing its base are the words: "those who cannot remember the past are condemned to repeat it." On Columbus Day, various patriotic organizations pay tribute to their favorite explorer at the Columbus Piazza **(below)**, dedicated in 1984 as the city's third memorial to the bold navigator.

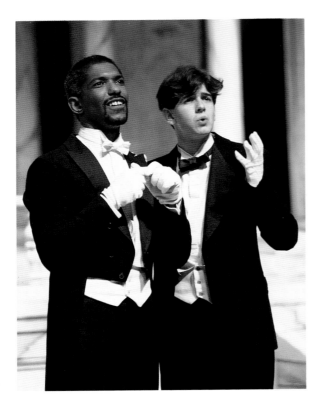

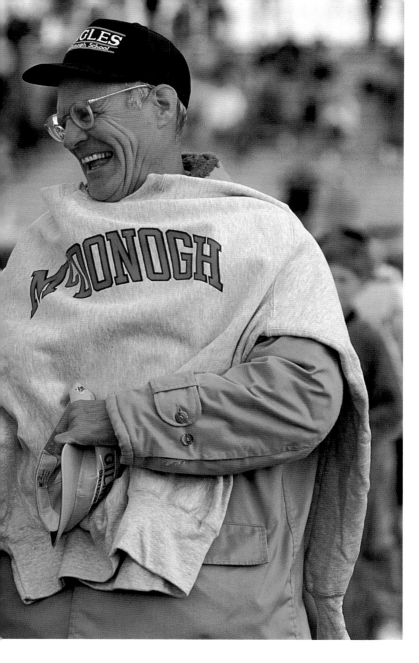

Baltimore is distinguished with a number of excellent schools, where colorful traditions have left their mark through the generations. **Clockwise:** At the Bryn Mawr School, girls perform European country dances during the annual Gym Drill. Students of the Baltimore Polytechnic Institute celebrate a touchdown at Memorial Stadium. At the Calvert School, each day commences with a firm handshake between the headmaster and all 387 students. Roses in hand, seniors at Roland Park Country School smile for a final class portrait on graduation day. Budding actors at the Baltimore School for the Arts perform Shakespeare's The Two Gentlemen of Verona. Finally, on the 75th anniversary of the McDonogh-Gilman football game in 1989, Al Levy (on the left), dean of McDonogh School from 1952 to 1986, exchanges pleasantries with long-time friend Reddy Finney, headmaster of Gilman School from 1968 to 1992.

Above: *Twin toddlers sport their Easter best at the New Psalmist Baptist Church. Founded in 1899, the church moved to its present downtown location — the former Franklin Street Presbyterian Church — in 1978, making it the first black church to join the cluster of prominent downtown churches. Like Bethel AME and other leading African-American churches, New Psalmist has taken an active role in the community, wielding considerable political influence and channeling its resources into programs which address the people's needs. Besides food and clothing, New Psalmist assists with college scholarships, job placement, counseling for substance abusers, and housing referrals.*

Left: *Worshippers at the Bethel African Methodist Episcopal Church celebrate their faith beneath a stunning mural depicting the advancement of African-Americans from the shackles of slavery. With a dwindling membership numbering several hundred in the 1970s, Bethel has been transformed into a prominent institution in the community, largely due to the efforts of its tireless leaders. Membership now exceeds 8,000. When the pews and balconies fill up before the Sunday services, congregants overflow into rooms equipped with closed-circuit television, while still others view emotional services from their homes during broadcasts on local television. Bethel is Maryland's oldest organized black church, tracing its congregation back to 1785, when a Bethel Free Africa Society was formed.*

Just another day at the office for a duo of daring window washers, who entrust their lives to thick ropes and well-tied

knots. Like most of Baltimore's large office buildings, Charles Center South needs a good bath about twice a year.

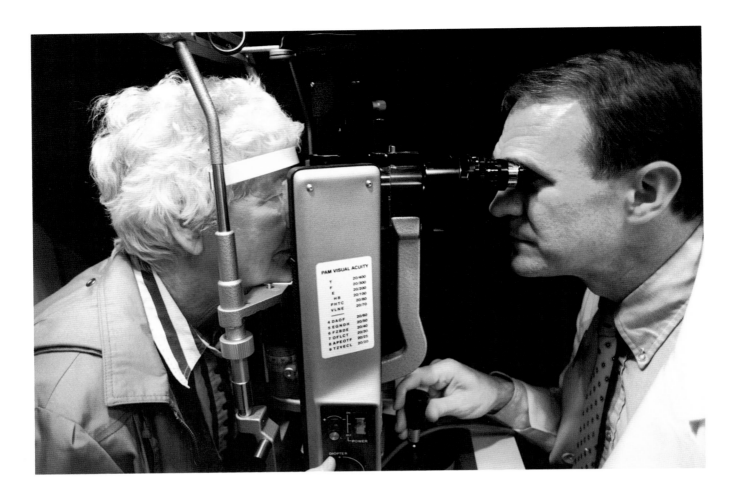

Johns Hopkins Hospital has emerged as a world leader in medical education, research, and treatment since it first opened its doors in 1889. The imposing marble statue of Christ known as Christus Consolator **(right)** dominates the rotunda of the magnificent Victorian administration building, offering comfort to countless thousands who pass by; some habitually rub the Divine Healer's toes for good luck. The Johns Hopkins Children's Center is Maryland's only acute-care hospital for children, treating some 7,000 inpatients annually in a number of facilities, like the neonatal intensive care unit **(below)** for premature infants and those with special medical problems. The Wilmer Eye Institute **(above)** was established in 1925 as the nation's first center devoted to the saving of vision; its pioneering techniques and discoveries have distinguished Wilmer as a preeminent eye research and treatment facility.

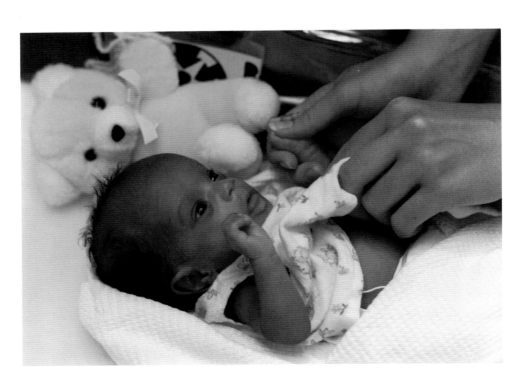

Above: Nestled along a steep river valley in eastern Howard County, historic Ellicott City is one of the most pleasant surprises of metropolitan Baltimore. Established in 1772 as Ellicott Mills, the town steadily grew as an industrial center with its flourishing mills along the Patapsco River. Today the well-preserved historic district is favored by tourists and shoppers, who are thoroughly charmed by its winding streets, fine shops, and restaurants.

Left: An aerial view of a Columbia neighborhood reveals a pleasant pattern of suburban development. Strategically located along the Baltimore-Washington corridor in Howard County, the city of Columbia represents one of the nation's largest — and most successful — planned communities. Since its inception in 1965 by visionary developer James Rouse, Columbia has grown under the guidance of the Rouse Company into an impressive city of 76,000 residents.

Above: Historic Davidge Hall landmarks the downtown campus of the University of Maryland at Baltimore, the founding campus of the statewide University of Maryland system. The university dates back to 1807 with the establishment of the state's first medical school; Davidge Hall is the original medical school building (1812). UMAB is currently comprised of seven schools—focused primarily on health care and human services—and of the University of Maryland Medical Center, a teaching hospital closely linked with the medical school.

Right: Gibbons Hall and its famed Merrick Tower anchor the campus of the College of Notre Dame, located just north of Loyola College. Distinguished among the nation's Catholic women's colleges as the first to grant the baccalaureate degree (1896), Notre Dame offers a strong liberal arts curriculum with an emphasis on moral and spiritual development. In addition, the college provides a Continuing Education Program for adult women, Weekend College for men and women employed full-time, and several graduate programs.

Left: The Alumni Chapel towers above the Evergreen campus of Loyola College in Maryland, one of the area's fastest growing colleges, located within the residential hub of North Baltimore. Founded in 1852 by the Jesuit Fathers, Loyola became fully coeducational in 1971 on merging with Mount Saint Agnes College. The 2,750 full-time students, representing all religious backgrounds, are challenged by a liberal arts curriculum; majors and minors are offered in more than thirty academic fields.

Above: The 30-story Commerce Place **(left of center)** takes shape as the latest addition to Baltimore's skyline. Despite a flurry of downtown redevelopment, the population of Baltimore City has been in decline for a number of years; with a population of 736,000 in 1990, it now ranks thirteenth among America's largest cities.

Left and Below: Shining jewel of Baltimore, the revitalized Inner Harbor is a magnet for tourists, and, once again, a bustling center of commerce. As recently as the early 1970s, the downtown waterfront was in a state of neglect and decay, abandoned by maritime merchants who retreated farther down the Patapsco. Well into its second decade, the renaissance has brought a wave of office buildings, hotels, restaurants, and tourist attractions. One of the latest additions is the Clarion Inn at Harrison's Pier 5, comprised of a hotel, shops, and the Eastern Shore Restaurant, opened in 1989 by the Harrison family of Tilghman Island. Pier 5 is also home to the Seven Foot Knoll Lighthouse, donated to the City of Baltimore in 1986 by the U.S. Coast Guard, and subsequently restored under the direction of the Lady Maryland Foundation.

Hopkins Plaza is a popular fair weather retreat for downtown office workers, especially at lunchtime. It is also the site of numerous community events, such as a demonstration by the Royal Lipizzaner Stallions of Austria **(left)** before an engagement at the Baltimore Arena. The focal point of the plaza is the Jacob France Memorial Fountain **(above)**, designed with soaring geysers to resemble a burst of fireworks. This urban park anchors the southern flank of Charles Center, a 33-acre complex of office buildings, highrise apartments, shops, restaurants, and the Morris A. Mechanic Theatre. This ambitious undertaking was launched in 1961 to help revive the city, and its success provided the energy and confidence to focus on the waterfront.

Above: *Highlandtowners seek relief from the relentless summer heat in their backyard pool, a fixture of East Baltimore. The common experiences of neighborhood living have woven a close-knit, fiercely proud community where families often live on the same block, if not the same row house, for generations. Baltimorese is the native language in this quintessential working-class neighborhood of formstone facades, white marble steps, and painted wire screens.*

Below: *Meat is ritualistically extracted from the Chesapeake blue crab at a summertime feast. Besides a love for the Orioles, an appetite for succulent crab meat serves as a unifying thread among Baltimoreans, regardless of social status. Nonetheless, there is no consensus as to what is the best way to eat a steamed crab. How about picking tidbits of meat from the skinny legs; is it really worth the trouble?*

Above: *Loyal customers of a Sandtown car wash, decorated wall-to-wall with 600 hubcaps and a 1950 Oldsmobile, watch the world pass by. This West Baltimore neighborhood is the focus of a multifaceted campaign — spearheaded by James Rouse and the Enterprise Foundation — to demonstrate to the country that poverty-stricken communities can be revitalized without burdening the taxpayer.*

Below: *A pedestrian along the 28th Street bridge has a close encounter with the jaws of death, thanks to the efforts of a local artist. Beginning in 1975, mural painting has decorated the city's face through the federally-funded Beautiful Walls for Baltimore program, designed to enliven drab and graffiti-marred public walls and to provide a boost for struggling artists. Supervised by the Mayor's Advisory Committee on Arts and Culture, this project has generated more than 100 works of art.*

Above: *Parishioners of the First and Franklin Street Presbyterian Church worship under a splendid triple-vaulted plaster ceiling. Also admired for its 273-foot steeple (Baltimore's tallest), this showcase of Victorian-Gothic architecture was built over a twenty-year period (1854-1874) as the new home of the First Presbyterian Church, which merged in 1973 with the Franklin Street Presbyterian Church.*

Right: *Mount Vernon Place United Methodist Church soars as one of the city's most handsome buildings, embellished with distinctive green serpentine marble. In 1870 a prime location was selected to build what would become the "Cathedral of Baltimore Methodism" — a corner of Mount Vernon Place, shadowed by George Washington atop his column, and the site where Francis Scott Key, author of the National Anthem, expired while visiting his daughter's house.*

Left: *Silent sentinels protrude from the enriched earth of Green Mount Cemetery, marking the final resting place of Marylanders celebrated and unsung. Established in 1838 as Baltimore's first rural cemetery, Green Mount was intended to attract overcrowded city dwellers for a day's outing, where they could enjoy the beautiful monuments and natural surroundings. More than 60,000 persons are buried here. Included among the scores of distinguished occupants are philanthropists Enoch Pratt, Johns Hopkins, and Henry and William Walters; the poet Sidney Lanier; photographer A. Aubrey Bodine; and the infamous actor John Wilkes Booth.*

Following pages: *The maze of highway ramps in South Baltimore, linking I-395 with I-95, swirls with rush hour traffic.*

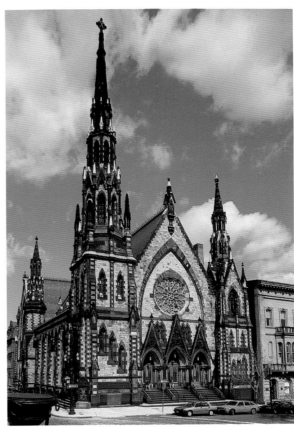

An assortment of architectural styles is reflected in the towers **(left)** of downtown Baltimore, including **(clockwise from bottom)** the Zion Lutheran Church, erected in 1807 and later expanded to include a parish hall; the splendid dome of City Hall, which rises above a three-story rotunda **(above)**, ringed by magnificent marble columns and capped by an interior dome; the 34-story Maryland National Bank building, completed in 1929 as Baltimore's tallest skyscraper; and the needle-like Merritt Tower, which caps off 6 St. Paul Centre.

Economic lifeline to Maryland, the Port of Baltimore is one of America's busiest deepwater ports, servicing more than 2,000 ships annually, which link Baltimore with some 100 seafaring nations. Compared to other East Coast ports, Baltimore enjoys the geographical advantage of being the closest to the nation's industrial and agricultural heartland. The port handles a vast array of cargo along its forty-five miles of jagged Patapsco River shoreline, ranging from industrial machinery, automobiles, and chemicals to grain, coal, lumber, and even tourists, as more cruise lines are choosing Baltimore as a point of embarkation.

A visiting tall ship **(right)** recalls the glory days of Fells Point as a thriving maritime center renowned for its abundance of shipyards, which launched many a Baltimore clipper ship. This remarkably well preserved port town, annexed by Baltimore in 1773, is one of the city's most illustrious neighborhoods. Some 350 residential structures from the early republic remain, to the delight of those who stroll along its Belgian-blocked streets. One of Fells Point's notable characters is Stevens Bunker **(above)**, proprietor of an unusual nautical salvage shop, the China Sea Marine Trading Company.

Above and below: *A fall victim arrives at the rooftop heliport of the R Adams Cowley Shock Trauma Center and is whisked to a trauma team in the ten-bay admitting area. Located on the University of Maryland at Baltimore campus, Shock Trauma is the nucleus of a statewide emergency medical network which links rescue teams, hospitals, and specialized medical centers throughout Maryland. The med-evac helicopter fleet, operated by the Maryland State Police, is a vital link in a system designed to provide treatment during the "golden hour" following traumatic injury, when immediate care is often the difference between life and death. Nine out of ten victims treated at Shock Trauma survive.*

Left: *Apprentice firefighters battle a house fire as part of the Baltimore County Fire Academy's controlled burning program. This innovative training exercise involves the leveling of properties slated for development, thus providing invaluable firsthand experience for trainees while sparing builders the cost of demolition. The academy is also nationally recognized for its success in tackling the problems of integrating both volunteer and career firemen within the same department.*

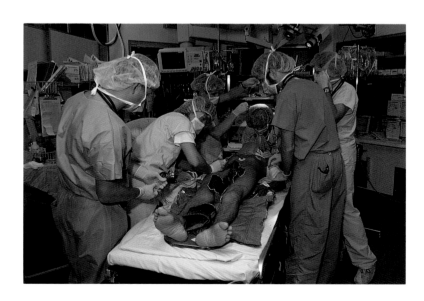

Above: The Baltimore County Courthouse, recently restored to its original grandeur, proudly stands as Towson's most recognizable landmark. This Greek revival edifice, with its handsome portico and cupola, was built in 1854 when Towson officially became the Baltimore County seat; it currently houses offices for county officials.

Right: A sculpted sea horse and eagle grace the entrance to the War Memorial Building, dedicated in 1925 as a tribute to Marylanders who served their country in World War I, and subsequently rededicated to honor veterans of following wars.

Below: The handsome clock of Pennsylvania Station hints of the splendor that lies within; opened in 1911 and currently owned by Amtrak, Pennsylvania Station is Baltimore's last grand railroad station still in use.

Left: At the Clarence Mitchell, Jr., Courthouse in downtown Baltimore, the halls of justice are as beautiful to architecture buffs as they are foreboding to those who break the law. In addition to twin Victorian stained-glass skylights, this monolithic building (opened in 1900) is noted for its colored marbles, imposing bronze doors, mahogany woodwork, and large murals depicting historical events and figures.

A majestic old barn along the Seminary Valley holds its ground against a wave of development which swells across the

gentle landscape of Baltimore County. Unfortunately, this Lutherville landmark burned down in 1992.

Above: Final preparations are made on masterpieces displayed for an open house through the kitchens of the Baltimore International Culinary College in downtown Baltimore. Acknowledged as one of America's premier international hospitality colleges, BICC offers two-year programs which prepare students for careers in the food service and lodging industries. Since 1987, students have received a portion of their training at the college's European Educational Centre in Ireland.

Below and right: Respected nationally as a leader in its field, the Maryland Institute, College of Art, offers professional training for visual artists, designers, and educators. The Institute was founded in 1826 as the nation's first four-year, degree-granting college of art. The diverse student body currently exceeds 800 talented artists, representing approximately forty states and forty-six nations. An unusual project recently hosted by the college is the sculpting of the world's largest Fudo Myoh-oh, a 33-foot "immovable king of light." The awesome Budda, completed in 1992, was crafted by several Japanese artists in a specially built studio. It is hoped that this fearsome sculpture will, in addition to intimidating evil spirits, help to bridge a wide cultural gap between the two countries.

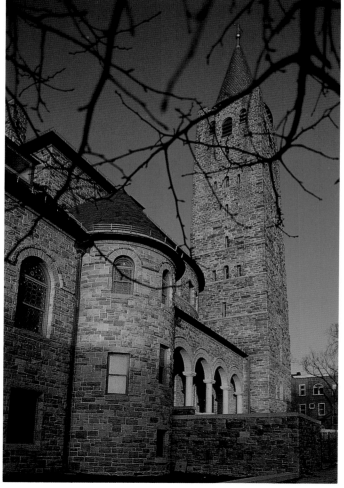

Top left: *University Baptist Church, completed in 1927 as relative newcomer on the church scene, was designed by the renowned architect John Russell Pope, whose classical buildings grace both Baltimore and the nation's capital.*

Bottom left: Lovely Lane United Methodist Church, hailed as the "Mother Church of American Methodism," stands as a stunning centennial monument to the national organization of the Methodist Episcopal Church in Baltimore in 1784. Lovely Lane also contains a museum of Methodism.

Above: The Lloyd Street Synagogue, built in 1845 as Maryland's first synagogue (the nation's third oldest remaining), anchors the Jewish Heritage Center in downtown Baltimore, which also includes a museum, library, and the B'Nai Israel Synagogue. The carefully restored Lloyd Street Synagogue is now a museum building, where visitors learn first-hand about Jewish culture.

Above: Tugboats assist the goliath USNS Comfort as she departs Baltimore (her home since 1988) for sea trials. Known as the "floating hospital," the 894-foot Comfort operates primarily as a full-service medical treatment facility (including 1,000 beds and 50 trauma stations) in support of military forces deployed in areas of imminent hostilities.

Below: A MARC train awaits passengers at the historic Camden Station, opened in 1857 as a terminal and headquarters for the Baltimore & Ohio Railroad. The Maryland Rail Commuter Service runs commuter trains on weekdays through the heavily-trafficked Baltimore-Washington corridor, and recently added service during baseball games. Rising in the background is the Baltimore Arts Tower — also known as the Bromo Seltzer Tower — built in 1911 for the Emerson Drug Company.

Left: A harvest moon glows through the Francis Scott Key Memorial Bridge, opened in 1977 as the long-awaited outer harbor crossing — and final link of the Baltimore Beltway — between Sollers and Hawkins Points. At the center of the 1.6 mile span across the Patapsco River, Baltimore City, Baltimore County, and Anne Arundel County intersect, approximately 100 yards from the spot where the bridge's honoree witnessed the British bombardment of Fort McHenry in 1814.

Above: *The National Aquarium glows at dusk as the most distinct building on Baltimore's urban landscape. Positioned at the center of the harbor on Piers 3 and 4, the National Aquarium has come to symbolize the "Renaissance City" with its bold, striking design.*

Left: *A departing tall ship measures high against the 30-story World Trade Center — the nation's tallest pentagonal building — completed in 1977 as a center for international commerce.*

Right: *Looking west from Highlandtown, one sees a hodgepodge of architectural works which constitute most of Baltimore's skyline. This same view just nineteen years ago would have included just one of the nine major buildings pictured in this scene.*

Above: Officers of the Baltimore City Police Department's Mounted Division survey the urban terrain amidst soaring towers of the financial district. Once relegated to policing downtown traffic, the Mounted Division has been rejuvenated through an expanded role of patrolling crime-ridden neighborhoods, where even the fastest thief or drug dealer is no match for a horse.

Right: When the mercury tops 100°F, neighborhood fire hydrants are recruited to provide some relief from the stifling heat. Children frolic in the streets—until the police show up — and sometimes offer free car washes, whether you want one or not; motorists who pass by with their windows down are in for quite a surprise.

Left: In East Baltimore pastoral painted screens have become a welcome complement to the ubiquitous rows of white marble steps. Quite decorative in an otherwise monotonous urban setting, painted screens are also functional. While the bugs are kept out, doors and windows can be left open for ventilation during sweltering summers without sacrificing privacy. Because the screens have a one-way viewing effect homeowners can see out through the unpainted side but curious sidewalk pedestrians see only a red-roofed cottage in an alpine setting (the most popular motif).

A fresh blanket of snow drapes the picturesque 835-acre campus of the McDonogh School in Owings Mills. Watching over the Allan Building is the McDonogh Monument, a handsome tribute to the school's founder, John McDonogh. Since it first opened in 1873 as a boarding school for orphans, McDonogh has grown into the largest independent school in Maryland, with an enrollment of some 1,170 students.

Williams Hall anchors the suburban campus of the Boys' Latin School of Maryland, located since 1960 on a former country estate in north Roland Park. Founded in 1844 by Evert Marsh Topping, a distinguished professor of Classics at Princeton University, Boys' Latin educates some 470 boys from kindergarten through grade twelve.

Lower School students of the Friends School of Baltimore enjoy a break from academic pursuits in the autumn sun. Baltimore's oldest school, Friends was established in 1784 by the Religious Society of Friends (Quakers). Though students represent a variety of religious backgrounds, all participate in a tradition called the Meeting for Worship (held at the adjacent Stony Run Friends Meeting), which consists of silent meditation and inspired spoken words.

The St. Paul's Center for the Arts, opened in the spring of 1992, highlights the 97-acre campus in Brooklandville shared by St. Paul's School and St. Paul's School for Girls. The $5.5 million center is jointly owned and operated by each school, featuring a 325-seat theatre, classrooms, studios, galleries, and a dining hall. Both schools trace thier origins to Old St. Paul's Church in downtown Baltimore; the boys' school still provides the choir for Sunday services.

Above: The twin arcades of Harborplace — the Light Street and Pratt Street Pavilions — offer a shopping extravaganza with more than 100 specialty shops, eateries, and restaurants. Orchestrated by developer James Rouse, the $18 million project came to fruition in 1980, when a staggering 150,000 visitors flocked to the Inner Harbor on its opening day. This waterfront gamble has paid off handsomely; according to Rouse Company estimates, nearly 200 million visitors have strolled the promenades and sun-filled pavilions of Harborplace in its first decade of operation.

Right: Paddleboats are a favorite way to see the sights of the Inner Harbor.

Left: Thousands enjoy an explosive Fourth of July celebration at the Inner Harbor. The rejuvinated waterfront, which finally took root in the early 1980s with the opening of Harborplace and the National Aquarium, has uplifted the spirits of an entire city. In the foreground is the World Trade Center, which offers tourists the Top of the World, a public observation deck featuring sweeping views of the city and exhibits relating to Baltimore's history.

Preceding pages: Mimes work their magic for a crowd at Artscape, one of Baltimore's most popular street festivals.

Above: Finishing touches are placed on the unusual set of The Mystery of Irma Vep, an engaging Center Stage production staged in the intimate Head Theatre. This flexible second performance space, opened in 1991, features movable seating towers. Created in 1963, Center Stage has established itself as a premier professional resident theatre, now in its third location, a renovated school building in Mount Vernon.

Below: The Lyric Opera House brims with passion during a Baltimore Opera Company presentation of Salome. The company was founded in 1950 under the direction of Rosa Ponselle, the celebrated Metropolitan Opera diva who settled in Baltimore. Though opera is still sung in a foreign language, English surtitles are now projected above the stage, broadening the appeal of this elite form of entertainment.

Right: Ziegfeld girls prepare to take the stage of Ziegfeld: A Night at the Follies, presented at the Morris A. Mechanic Theatre by the non-profit Baltimore Center for the Performing Arts. Recognized as one of the country's most progressive legitimate theatres, the Mechanic opened in 1968 as a centerpiece of the Charles Center revitalization effort, hosting Broadway musicals, comedies and dramas.

Above: Muskets erupt as British troops engage the Americans during a re-enactment of the Battle of North Point. On landing near what is now Fort Howard in Baltimore County, the British advance during the War of 1812 was challenged by a formidable local militia. A hasty retreat ended the land campaign, and British hopes then rested on the naval attack on Fort McHenry.

Right: The Civil War Living History Weekend at Ballestone Manor in Essex provides a unique opportunity to experience this troubled era of American history. Visitors may witness various facets of a soldier's life, from meals around the campfire to agony on the battlefield. It is no wonder that some soldiers sneak a quick nap during this action-packed weekend.

Above and below: Scores of bars make Fells Point one of the wettest watering holes anywhere, and bar hopping among a host of trendy bars has become a virtual rite of passage for many Baltimoreans. Known for their sometimes colorful signs, the pubs of Fells Point have been quenching thirsts for more than two centuries. On Halloween, the streets crawl with an eye-opening assortment of characters.

Left: Young upwardly-mobile professionals celebrate the weekend's arrival along Water Street Mews, where the bars host one of Baltimore's happiest Happy Hours. With finishing touches like cobblestones and old fashioned lampposts, the restoration of this half-block of Water Street is a pleasant surprise for travelers along Light Street, which it intersects.

Following pages: Children from the Bethel Korean School perform a striking Puppet Dance before a crowd at Hopkins Plaza during the annual Korean Festival.

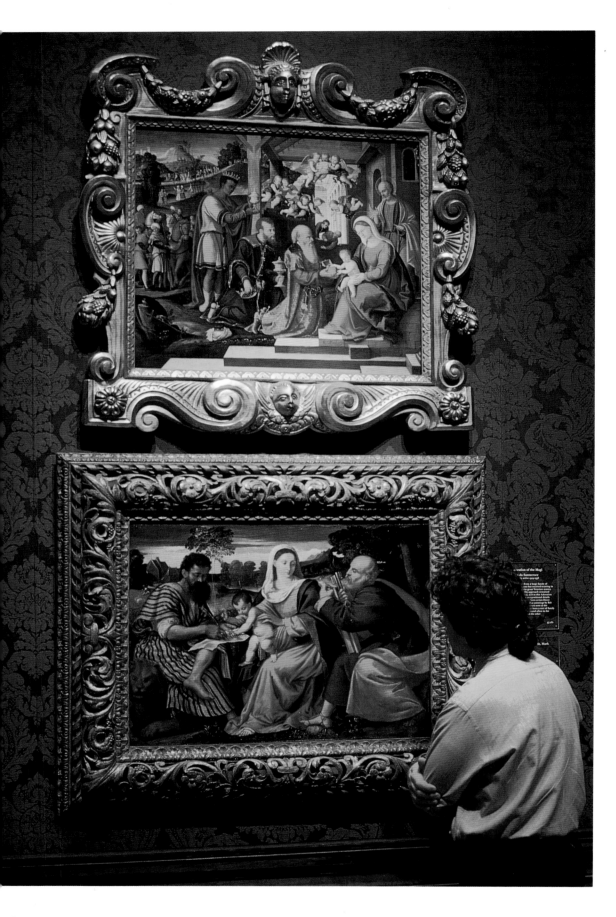

The magnificent displays of the Walters Art Gallery showcase a portion of the museum's 30,000 objects, ranging from ancient Egypt to art nouveau. The original art gallery (1904), home to the Old Masters paintings **(above)**, was designed in the Italian Renaissance revival style; its central court **(top)** replicates the seventeenth century Palazzo Balbi in Genoa, Italy. In 1974 a modern four-story wing was added to house ancient, medieval, and nineteenth century art **(right)**. The Walters came into public service through an act of grand philanthropy: local art connoisseur Henry Walters bequeathed his gallery and collections — assembled with his father, William — to the city upon his death in 1931.

Let the parade begin! At the annual Columbus Day Parade a young girl from a local Columbia club **(above)** patiently awaits the start of the nation's largest parade to honor the fearless explorer. Maria Broom's Keiki Wahini **(left)**, performing dances of Hawaii, Jamaica, and the Far East, takes part in the Afram Festival kick-off parade.

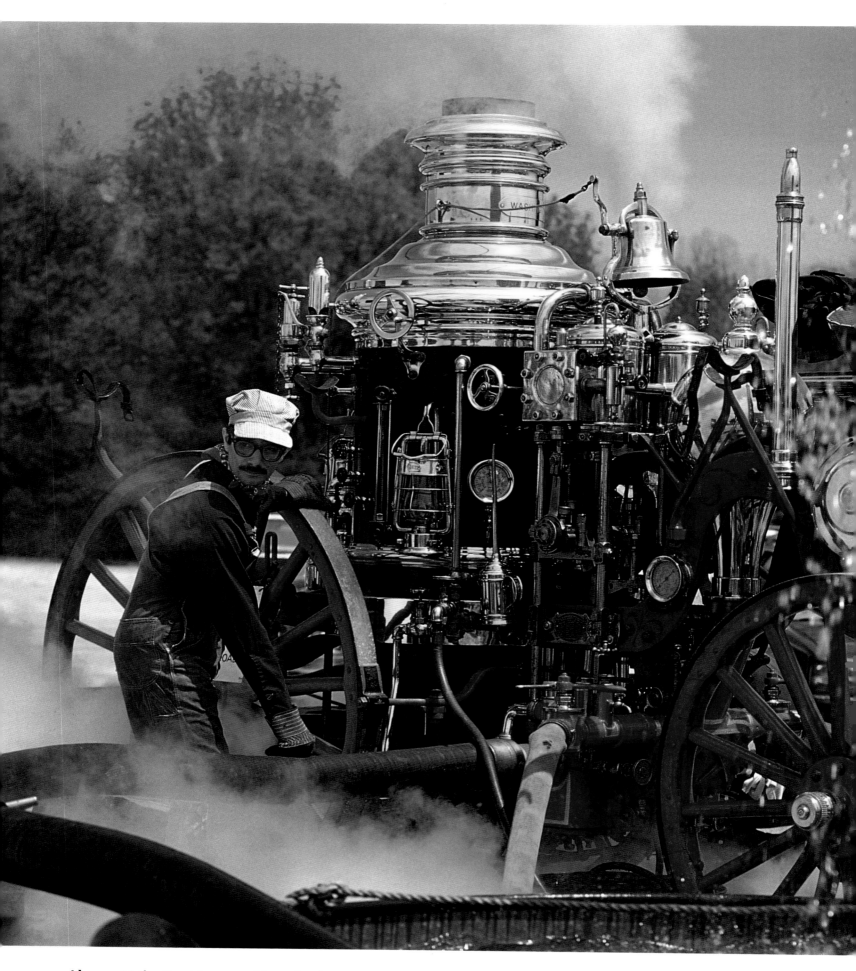

Above: *At the Fire Museum of Maryland, a vintage pumping engine is called into service during the annual Steam Sunday celebration each May, when volunteers demonstrate how various fire-fighting apparatus work. More than sixty vehicles and displays of related equipment make this Lutherville attraction one of the country's finest fire museums.*

Right: *Glimpses of the city's colorful history are kept alive by the Baltimore City Life Museums, a network of six attractions. A resurrected H.L. Mencken* **(top)** *— known as the "Sage of Baltimore" and "Attila of Critics" — outwits guests in his beloved garden behind 1524 Hollins Street, one of America's premier literary addresses. In the 1840 House courtyard* **(bottom)**, *friends discuss Christmas plans. This museum is dedicated to living history, recreating daily experiences of a typical family.*

Above: *A bargain hunter has staked his claim to a bust at Connoisseur's Collection, one of some thirty shops that comprise historic Antique Row. Concentrated along two blocks of North Howard Street, Maryland's oldest antiques shopping district offers a full range of objects d'art — everything from medieval to art deco.*

Below: *The vintner's latest offering awaits eager palates at Boordy Vineyards in Hydes. At the forefront of Maryland's burgeoning wine industry — in a climate well-suited for the cultivation of grapes — Boordy produces over 18,000 gallons of wine annually.*

Right: *The spectacular Rotunda atrium court, capped by a massive vaulted dome, highlights the expanded Towson Town Center. Styled with elaborate flourishes designed to evoke the formal gardens of classical Europe, suburban Baltimore's glitziest mall offers nearly 200 specialty stores on four levels and the area's first Nordstrom department store.*

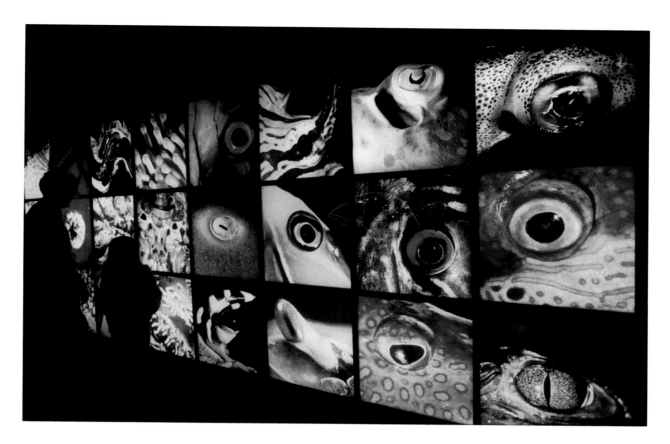

The National Aquarium in Baltimore is one of the nation's most exciting aquaria, showcasing more than 5,000 creatures and plants from marine environments across the globe. In 1990 the Marine Mammal Pavilion **(top left)** opened as a magnificent addition, featuring a 1,300-seat amphitheater where spectators are treated to demonstrations of its agile bottlenose dolphins and beluga whales, which are currently out on breeding loan. The National Aquarium offers unusual displays which immerse the viewer into the marine world; one such exhibit is a series of brilliant panels **(above)** which graphically depict various adaptations of marine creatures. The glass pyramid roof of the aquarium shelters a living rain forest, home to such free-moving residents as the scarlet ibis **(below)**. Other colorful residents include the Navarchus angelfish **(bottom left)**, the hawksbill sea turtle **(below)** and the blue poison dart frog **(below)**.

Distinguished vessels which have been retired to Baltimore are a big draw at the Inner Harbor. Billed as the world's oldest continuously afloat warship, the U.S. Frigate Constellation **(above)** proudly served her country through nearly 150 years of conflict. Since this oldest ship of the U.S. Navy returned to Baltimore in 1955, controversy has surrounded her authenticity, but that does not stop the 200,000 visitors who pay her tribute annually. A prized possession of the Baltimore Museum of Industry, the 1906 steam tug Baltimore **(right)** fires her engines. Salvaged from the Sassafras River bottom in 1981, the Baltimore is undergoing a complete restoration, so that she may once again work the harbor, this time as a tour boat. Moored alongside the National Aquarium is the fearsome submarine Torsk **(left)**, operated by the Baltimore Maritime Museum. Not only did the Torsk fire the last torpedoes of World War II, but she made a record 11,884 dives.

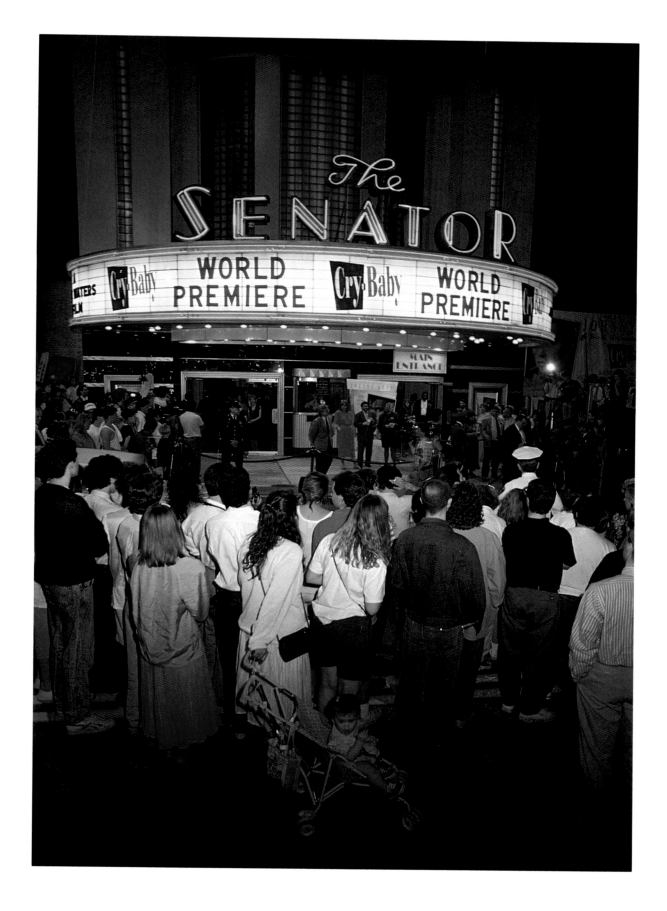

Above: *Fans hope to catch a glimpse of the stars as they arrive at the world premier of John Waters' Cry-Baby, hosted by the Senator Theatre. Celebrating its 50th birthday in 1989, this illustrious movie house is Baltimore's sole survivor from a golden era when going to the movies was an experience unto itself, as glamorous movie palaces gave the public a taste of the high life. The Senator, styled with an art deco flare, has also provided its patrons a glimpse of Hollywood during other special premiers, including Diner, Hairspray, The Accidental Tourist, and Avalon.*

Left: *A derelict building in Fells Point is given a facelift as a brand new department store during the filming of Avalon, released to a national audience in 1990. Written and directed by Barry Levinson, Baltimore's mainstream cinematic ambassador, the film chronicles the assimilation of a Russian immigrant family into American society over several generations. Like Diner and Tin Men, also directed by Levinson, Avalon celebrates the hometown of its Oscar-winning director.*

As Baltimore has been celebrated for more than a century for its wonderful foods — especially delicacies from the Chesapeake Bay — one would expect a gamut of fine restaurants, and that expectation is fulfilled in Charm City. Often voted Baltimore's best restaurant is Tio Pepe **(above right)** a true classic enticing gourmands for decades with succulent Spanish cuisine. Another elegant restaurant is the Conservatory **(right)**, a sumptuous Victorian parlor perched atop the Peabody Court Hotel, offering French cuisine and unrivaled panoramic views of the city. Perhaps the most famous of the favorites is Haussner's **(above)**, where diners feast on German-American entrees amidst Baltimore's largest privately-owned art collection — representing some 300 artists — displayed profusely throughout the dining rooms. A landmark on the neighborhood crab house scene is Old Obrycki's **(left)**, where the steamed crabs are piled high.

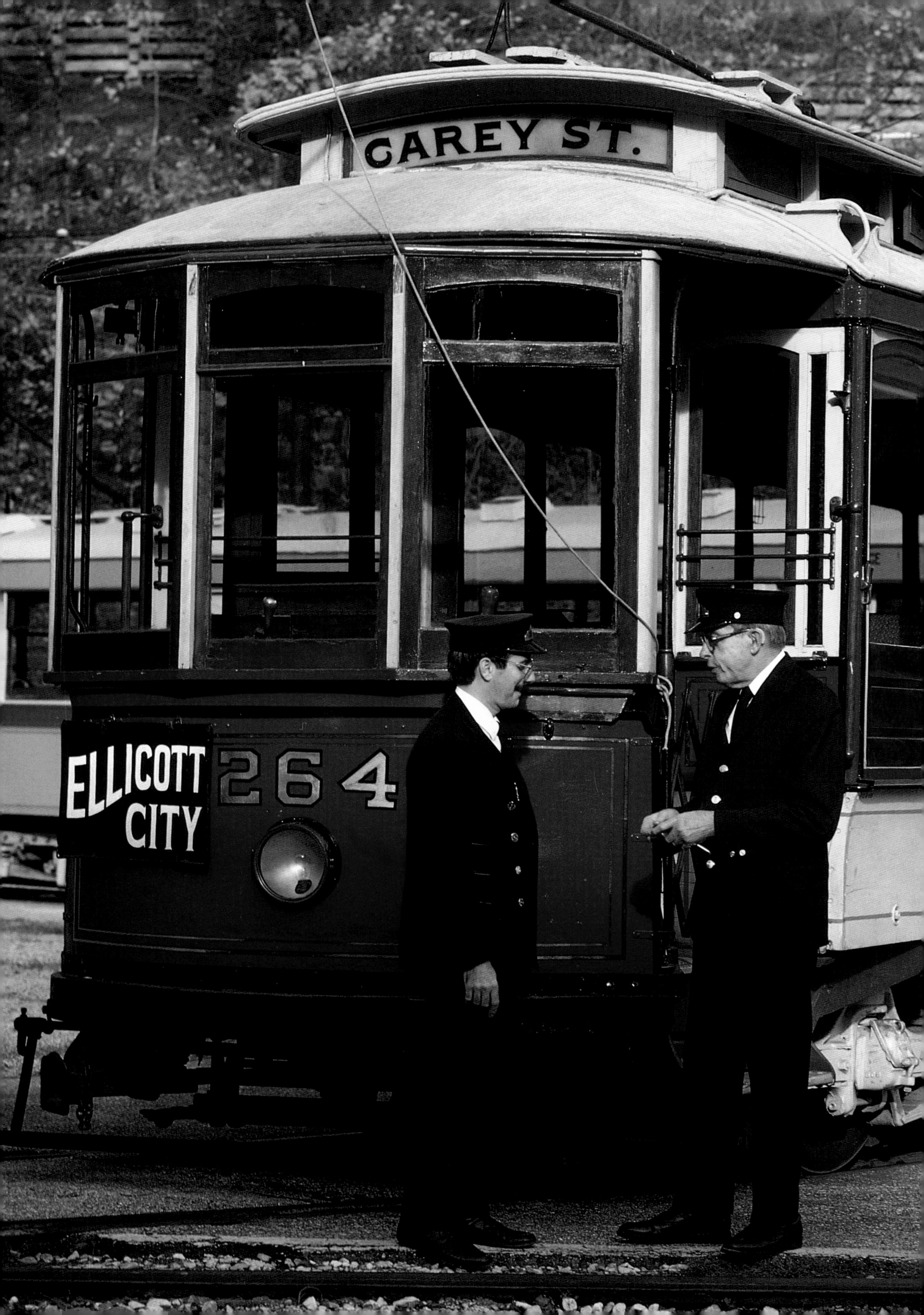
CAREY ST.
ELLICOTT CITY
264

Above: The B&O Railroad Museum displays America's finest collection of railroading artifacts and memorabilia, chronicling more than 160 years of train history. Featured are some eighty freight and passenger cars and steam and diesel locomotives, the rarest of which are displayed in the Roundhouse, a 22-sided building (almost round) erected in 1884 as a repair shop. The museum also includes Mount Clare Station, the nation's first passenger terminal (1829) of the pioneering Baltimore & Ohio Railroad.

Left: Conductors converse at the Baltimore Streetcar Museum, located along Falls Road in the Lower Jones Falls Valley. Following the installation of the first rails in 1859, streetcars became a vital force behind the transformation of Baltimore from a harborside town to a sprawling metropolis. As the last streetcar was retired in 1963, the museum provides a nostalgic link to this golden era of public transportation, where visitors can step back in time by riding on a recreated streetcar line.

Above, below, and right: Some of the biggest acts in entertainment make an appearance at the Baltimore Arena, including the Harlem Globetrotters, the Moscow Circus, and the Ice Capades. Some 220 events are staged annually at this 14,000-seat forum.

Left: A lady with a magical smile glides across the Inner Harbor Ice Rink during an 1860s skate in honor of Lincoln's Birthday. This festive event was one of many offered during the three-month Baltimore On Ice celebration, held in 1989 and 1990 to provide entertainment on a public skating rink.

Courtesy of the dedicated volunteers of Baltimore Operation Sail, this great port city has played host to a number of the world's majestic tall ships, including the Libertad **(above)** of Argentina, and the spectacular Italian naval training vessel Amerigo Vespucci **(left)**. A non-profit group, Operation Sail was formed in 1975 to attract a variety of international ships, primarily to boost tourism and the local economy. One year later a reported two million people flocked to the Inner Harbor to witness an awesome assemblage of eight tall ships which had participated in the nation's 1976 Bicentennial celebration in New York City. Since its inception, Operation Sail has brought more than 200 ships to Baltimore.

Following pages: The night sky blazes as spinning wheels twirl thrill seekers at the Maryland State Fair in Timonium, a favorite family outing since 1878.

Above: Some 100,000 lights shimmer at a private home on Frog Mortar Road in Middle River. This annual Christmas display — complete with angels, carolers, toy soldiers, gingerbread men, reindeer, santas, and a manger scene — is one of several in the area that draw an annual pilgrimage. The crawling queue with carloads of peering eyes is welcome to make contributions at this display, which are then donated by the owner to the Johns Hopkins Children's Center.

Right: A biker with a big heart presents his ticket to the annual Motorcyclist's Operation Santa Claus gathering, begun in 1981 to benefit needy families in the Baltimore area. Donations from the more than 65,000 bikers — representing all walks of life — fill several large trailers with a myriad of Christmas presents, later distributed by the Salvation Army.

Left: Leprechauns from the senior and junior divisions await the competition during a leprechaun look-alike contest, part of the St. Patrick's Day Celebration at Broadway Market Square in Fells Point. Under the direction of Virginia Baker, appointed in 1973 by Mayor Schaefer as Baltimore's First Lady of Fun, the Office of Adventures in Fun sponsors this and other holiday festivities, in addition to activities at the Recreation Pier in Fells Point.

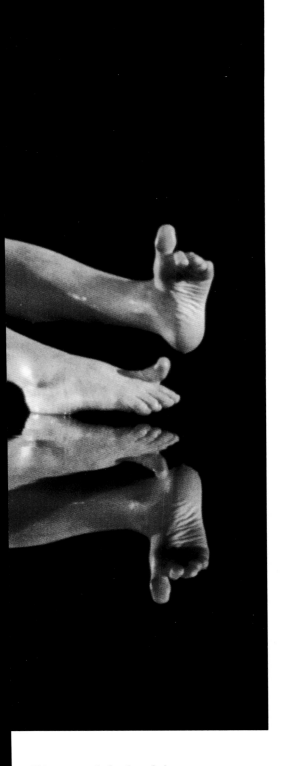

Glimpses of the local dance scene show a variety of electrifying performances. Maureen Fleming **(above)** performs Water on the Moon, an unusual, slightly eerie dance which explores the universal development of the soul. Since 1987, the Downtown Dance Company has sponsored such contemporary performances as part of their Dance on the Edge series. A fast-paced Spanish dancer **(right)** is frozen in time during a public dance concert staged by the Peabody Preparatory, a community school which currently provides some 2,000 children and adults quality instruction in dance and music. The Maryland Ballet performs a holiday classic, The Nutcracker **(left).** Founded in 1986 as the Harbor City Ballet—the state's only professional ballet company — the Maryland Ballet presents both a classical and contemporary repetoire, including original works by Artistic Director Phillip Carmen.

Top: Mount Clare stands tall as Baltimore's sole surviving pre-Revolutionary building and as the nation's only existing colonial plantation within city limits. Completed in 1760, this Georgian mansion anchored the 800-acre Patapsco River plantation of Charles Carroll the Barrister and his wife. Many original furnishings and collections are displayed throughout the recently restored rooms and hallways, providing a glimpse of life in early America.

Above: Hampton Mansion serves as an elegant reminder of an era when gentrified living took on magnificent proportions. Praised as one of the country's finest examples of Georgian architecture, Hampton was constructed between 1783 and 1790 as the centerpiece of a 24,000-acre empire of agriculture, industry, and commerce, amassed by the Ridgely family in Baltimore County. Since 1948 the site has been managed by the National Park Service.

Left: The spectacular portico of Evergreen hints of the cultural and architectural treasures that lay within. Originally built in the 1850s overlooking the ever-fashionable Charles Street, the grand house became a symbol of opulence with the lavish additions and remodeling by two generations of the Garrett family. Evergreen's forty-eight rooms showcase valuable collections of oriental art, early twentieth century paintings, and rare books.

The Baltimore Zoo celebrates the diversity of animal life found throughout the earth's seven continents with more than 1,200 mammals, birds, and reptiles. Unforgettable sights include **(clockwise)** the Siberian tiger, green tree python, common zebra, lesser flamingo, reticulated giraffe, African crowned crane, and polar bear. Set on 150 acres of wooded hills in Druid Hill Park, the nation's third oldest zoo has upgraded and expanded its exhibits in recent years, providing natural habitats which instill a sense of environment and conservation. At the Maryland Wilderness area **(left)** of the new Children's Zoo, interactive exhibits offer youngsters a unique opportunity to sample indigenous wildlands.

141

Above: *Heavy metal band Poison rocks a capacity crowd at Hammerjacks, Baltimore's legendary night club, whose reputation extends far beyond Maryland's borders. Located in an old brewery building next to the new ballpark, Hammerjacks is the area's premier rock and roll concert venue, staging an average of three concerts per week, featuring a mix of local and national bands. In 1991 a second concert hall was added to handle larger crowds. The favorite drink at the club's fourteen bars is still Budweiser, but the clientele of Hammerjacks is broadening from its traditionally blue-collar regulars. To the regret of some, the ever popular wet T-shirt, naughty negligee, and macho man contests are being phased out.*

Left: *John Taylor enthusiastically leads an "Electric Slide" dance in the streets of the Mount Royal cultural corridor during Artscape, Baltimore's annual celebration of the arts. Held each July since 1981, this three-day festival showcases the talents of local and national artists with a variety of outdoor and indoor visual arts exhibitions, music and dance performances, literary readings, street performances, crafts and food, and special activities for children. Crowds measured in the thousands enjoy Artscape free of charge, thanks to tremendous support from individuals, foundations, corporations, and government agencies.*

Above and right: Under the leadership of Music Director David Zinman, the Baltimore Symphony Orchestra is cherished as one of Baltimore's most dynamic cultural institutions. Since 1982 the Joseph Meyerhoff Symphony Hall has been home to the BSO, which celebrated its 75th birthday in 1991. Located within the Mount Royal cultural corridor, the uniquely designed hall is renowned for its superior acoustics, achieved partially through a series of convex curves which transmit sound more effectively. The BSO gives some 125 concerts a year in the elegant Meyerhoff Hall, where all 2,470 seats offer an unobstructed view of the stage.

Left: The glory days of ballroom dancing return to the Engineering Society of Baltimore at Mount Vernon Place. This prestigious society arose from the catastrophic Great Fire of 1904 when a group of engineers organized to help rebuild Baltimore. Since its founding in 1905, the society has had a number of homes, and in 1963 it purchased as its permanent home the Garrett-Jacobs Mansion, the most luxurious townhouse in Victorian Baltimore. The Auditorium, originally built as an ornate art gallery and ballroom, is used to provide both educational and social programs for its members.

Santa Claus and the First Lady of the North Pole offer holiday cheer during their annual debut at the Thanksgiving Day Parade **(above)** in downtown Baltimore, where they take a month-long residency at Santa's Place **(right)**. At this glittering palace by the harbor, children can place their Christmas orders early and have their pictures snapped with a jolly St. Nick.

Following pages: In the wake of Harborplace's success, the Rouse Company opened the Gallery in 1987, a six-level atrium of top flight shops, located opposite the Pratt Street Pavilion in the Legg Mason Tower complex.

Above: *A maritime historian brings to life the experiences of a nineteenth century sailor as part of the annual "Sealore Ashore" program at the Maryland Historical Society, founded in 1844. Located several blocks from Mount Vernon Place, the Society offers visitors extensive collections of furniture, paintings, silver, toys, costumes, ship models, books, and other treasures relating to the Free State's heritage.*

Right: *Constructed from more than one million bricks, the 215-foot Baltimore Shot Tower survives as a soaring relic of the city's grand industrial heritage. Shot was manufactured for shotgun and musket ammunition through the drop method: molten lead droplets would solidify as rounded pellets after being dropped through the tower's shaft into a quenching tank. Completed in 1828, the tower was one of America's top producers. Abandoned in 1892 and later rescued from destruction, this handsome landmark was converted into a museum in 1977 with various displays on its first floor.*

Left: *In a twist of irony, the Fort McHenry Guard offers a cordial salute from atop the ramparts to a visiting British warship. The stellar hallmark of the star-shaped fort — a massive replica of the 43-by-30-foot Star-Spangled Banner — flies day and night (weather permitting) by presidential decree. Fort McHenry earned an illustrious spot in history during the Battle of Baltimore (September 12-14, 1814) by withstanding a 25-hour British bombardment of some 1,800 bombs and rockets. Following the attack, a young Washington lawyer named Francis Scott Key, who had been detained on a British warship, was inspired at the sight of the American flag still flying over the fort. Key's poem became our National Anthem in 1931.*

Classic Baltimore shines her true colors in a host of ethnic festivals which feature music, food, dance, and other delights to the senses. Several ethnic groups participate in the city-coordinated Showcase of Nations, a summer-long series of festivals staged at Festival Hall and outdoor locations like Hopkins Plaza, site of the Korean Festival **(above)**, and Carroll Park, home to the German Festival **(lower right)**. In addition to these large-scale events, several groups also hold smaller, more intimate celebrations, reminiscent of the old days when neighborhood streets swelled with ethnic pride during informal gatherings. The St. Gabriel's Festival **(upper right)** in Little Italy is one such affair.

153

The Baltimore Museum of Art, seventy-five years old in 1989, houses Maryland's largest permanent collections of art — more than 130,000 objects, spanning five continents and nearly 4,000 years of human history. The prominent Cone Collection highlights the museum's early twentieth century works, including the paintings and sculptures of Renoir, Cezanne, van Gogh, Gaughin, and Picasso; Matisse's Blue Nude **(left)** is the collection's keystone piece. The BMA is also distinguished by its exhibits of American decorative arts; prints, drawings, and photographs; and the arts of Africa, the Americas, and Oceania. As part of an active acquisition and expansion campaign, the BMA purchased Andy Warhol's silk screen The Last Supper **(below)** in 1989. Special touring shows like the Monet Exhibition in 1992 also keep the BMA at the forefront of the museum world.

Colorful booths encircle the Washington
Monument on the occasion of the annual Flower
Mart, held on the first Wednesday each May. This
favorite rite of spring since 1911 offers fair
weather shoppers an abundance of flowers, treats
for the tastebuds, such as crab cakes and
peppermint lemon sticks, and hours of
entertainment, including a parade, maypole dance,
and organ recitals at the adjacent church.
Proceeds from this classic festival — sponsored
by the Women's Civic League — are donated
toward the preservation of historic Baltimore.

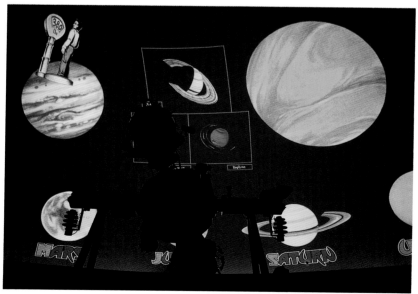

The Maryland Science Center **(above)** opened in 1976 as the first major attraction along the Inner Harbor waterfront; currently more than 500,000 guests annually immerse themselves in the fascinating world of science throughout three floors of interactive exhibits. A particular favorite is the hair-raising experiment on static electricity **(above right)**, one of several daily live science demonstrations. Special temporary exhibits such as Dinosaurs **(right)**, which brings one face to face with moving, talking beasts of the Mesozoic Era, provide a periodic change of scenery. The Maryland Science Center also boasts an IMAX Theatre, the world's largest motion picture system where spectators are drawn into the action, and the Davis Planetarium **(left)**, which transports guests to outer space under a 50-foot dome.

Top: *A new look is tried on for size at Octavia, one of several top flight clothing stores that makes the Village Square of Cross Keys in North Baltimore a highlight of the local shopping scene.*

Above: *Models sporting winter whites entertain holiday shoppers as snowflakes fall at Owings Mills Mall during a fashion show staged along the Grand Staircase. This upscale mall opened in 1985 with great fanfare as a cornerstone of the master development plan for the Owings Mills area of Baltimore County.*

Right: *The world premier of Hairspray at the Senator inspires local coiffeuses to knock themselves out with hairdos from yesteryear. Written, produced, and directed by John Waters, Baltimore's own controversial filmmaker, Hairspray is one of a string of Waters films, shot in and around Baltimore, which explore the sometimes unpleasant side of life. Other titles include* Pink Flamingos, Eat Your Makeup *and* Mondo Trasho.

Above: By the time the sun rises over the Middle Branch of the Patapsco, most crew teams are wrapping up their morning workouts, which may begin as early as 5:15 a.m. in a dark, bone-chilling cold. The grueling sport of rowing is alive and well in South Baltimore, where four local colleges and the 135-member Baltimore Rowing Club ply these rejuvenated waters year round. The rigorous training culminates in regattas staged each year at the Baltimore Rowing and Water Resource Center at Middle Branch Park.

Left: Robert E. Lee Park has become a favorite place for rest and relaxation, located just one mile north of the city near Ruxton. The imposing granite dam, built in 1861 to create a water supply for Baltimore, forms Lake Roland, which has since lost much of its capacity due to silt buildup. Today the area represents a rare suburban sanctuary, its varied habitat sheltering a host of wildlife. Bird life is especially abundant, and bird watchers regularly scour the woods and wetlands for representatives of the nearly 200 species that have been identified there.

Preceding pages: Thoroughbreds graze on the spacious fields of Ross Valley Farm in Baltimore County, perhaps the most picturesque of Maryland's nearly 900 horse farms.

Above: *Graceful thoroughbreds duel along the rail at Timonium Race Track during the ten days of racing coinciding with the Maryland State Fair. Maryland's passion for horse breeding and racing currently translates into a $1 billion industry, with 28,000 thoroughbreds in residence.*

Below: *A wave of runners rolls down Light Street at the start of the Constellation Classic 10K run. Held each Memorial Day Weekend since 1976 in downtown Baltimore, this popular race draws upwards of 3,000 participants; the most skilled runners complete the course in half an hour.*

Right: *Radiant hot-air balloons fill the sky to the delight of thousands of Baltimore's early risers. The Preakness Balloon Race highlights the city's biggest party: a ten-day celebration boasting more than 100 statewide events — everything from fancy balls to frog hops — which lead up to Preakness Day. This annual spectacle features some twenty-five balloons, which lift off from Druid Hill Park.*

Among the many spectacular birds that call Baltimore home are the barred owl **(left)**, snowy egret **(above)**, and wood duck **(below)**. Second only to the great horned owl in size, the barred owl is a common native species, and, like other owls, it is primarily a night hunter, relying on its supersensitive large eyes and acute sense of hearing, aided by distinct facial disks designed to detect even the faintest sounds. The beautiful white plumes of the snowy egret nearly spelled its demise, as these birds were once hunted extensively for their ornamental feathers. This egret is tending a nest in a protected rookery near the Patapsco River. The brilliant breeding plumage of the male wood duck marks it as one of the world's most handsome waterbirds. Unlike most other ducks, the wood duck prefers thick woods to open waters, and can be seen perched on tree limbs.

Above: The Chesapeake Rugby Club (in green) battles a team from a visiting British warship for a little weekend fun. Founded in 1969, this group of rugged architects, plumbers, lawyers, stockbrokers, and the like, primarily compete against Mid-Atlantic teams in the Potomac Rugby Conference. Home matches are played each spring and fall at the University of Baltimore Athletic Complex in Mount Washington.

Right: A near miss for a jouster competing in a tournament hosted by Mount Clare at Carroll Park. Maryland's official state sport is quite tame by medieval standards, when charging knights attempted to dismount each other. The contemporary, and more inviting version challenges the rider to lance nine rings (the size dependent on skill level) on three charges under a specified time limit.

The living classrooms of the Lady Maryland
Foundation offer area school children a unique
opportunity to learn about the local economy,
history, and ecology while sailing on the
Chesapeake Bay. Based in the 1856 Seven Foot
Knoll Lighthouse on Harrison's Pier 5, the
foundation currently uses two vessels for its
maritime programs, which educate more than
11,000 students annually through challenging
hands-on activities such as plotting and
navigating a course, preparing a daily weather
forecast, learning how to tie knots, and
identifying wildlife. The Lady Maryland **(right)**
was launched in 1986 as a replica of an 1880s
pungy schooner, used primarily to haul cargo on
the bay. Three years later the foundation
acquired the Mildred Belle **(below)**, an authentic
buy boat built in 1948.

Action at the ballpark heats up on special occasions when amateurs get into the swing of things. Former captain of the 1948 Yale baseball team, President George Bush **(right)** unleashes a not-so-fast fastball to commence the 1989 "Season of Dreams" at Memorial Stadium. From the disastrous season of 1988, which started out with an unprecedented twenty-one consecutive losses, the Baltimore Orioles rebounded with panache — holding first place for 116 days and almost winning their division. During Family Day for children of the Orioles, pitcher and hometown hero Dave Johnson stands behind his little slugger **(above)**, who goes for a high pitch.

Right: *Shooting for the gold, an energetic senior hurls a six pound shot during a track and field competition at the Maryland Senior Olympics. Staged each fall at Towson State University, the games draw as many as 1,500 athletes, aged fifty-five to over ninety, from all over the Free State. More than thirty events are offered to both men and women, ranging from a friendly game of horseshoes to an exhausting 10,000 meter run.*

Left: *Baltimore City College and the Baltimore Polytechnic Institute grind it out on the turf of Memorial Stadium on Thanksgiving Day during one of the city's greatest sporting traditions. This gridiron classic dates back to 1889 as the nation's second oldest scholastic rivalry; Poly has a slight edge with fifty wins, compared to forty-seven City victories.*

Left: *Ironmen charge the Gunpowder River in Baltimore County to start the Bud Light triathalon, comprised of a 1.5K swim, 40K bike race, and a 10K run which finishes at Rash Field in the Inner Harbor. The Baltimore event of this national triathalon series has attracted upwards of 2,000 men and women, making it the largest such competition in the Mid-Atlantic region.*

For nature lovers, the Baltimore area is a pleasant surprise, teeming with creatures large and small. Young opossums **(above)** cling for dear life as their mother traverses a log. This chiefly nocturnal species is North America's sole marsupial; the bee-size newborn must embark on a precarious journey to mother's pouch until development is completed in some sixty days. A monarch butterfly **(below)** feeds on the nectar of autumn flowers, building its energy reserve for an epic migration south of the border. Each fall millions of monarchs from North America travel to a remote wilderness area in Mexico, where they blanket the mountainsides during the winter. An inquisitive raccoon **(left)** glows in the beam of a flashlight. Equally at home in the forest or city alley, the omnivorous raccoon has gained notoriety for its nimble fingers, capable of reaching almost any meal.

Following pages: At Middle Branch Park anglers compete with crabbers for the bounty of the Chesapeake Bay; with a little skill and patience, a tasty dinner can be extracted from the calm waters. After decades of pollution and neglect, the Middle Branch of the Patapsco has been successfully reclaimed from near destruction, and it is now the focus of a popular city park.

Above and below: *Springtime splendor in Druid Hill Park promises restful moments for those seeking relief from the hustle and bustle of city life. In addition to a variety of recreational activities such as tennis, basketball, swimming, and gardening, the 675-acre Druid Hill Park is home to the Baltimore Zoo, a reservoir, and the Conservatory* **(above)**, *an elegant Victorian greenhouse built in 1888 to shelter exotic tropical flora, including rubber, banana, and palm trees; and desert and jungle plants, now contained in adjacent greenhouses.*

Right: *Youngsters celebrate school closing on the slopes of Patterson Park, 155 acres of fun — baseball diamonds, a duck pond, tennis courts, a swimming pool and ice skating rink, and outdoor concerts — amidst the neighborhoods of East Baltimore. Cresting the hill is the Patterson Park Observatory, a 60-foot octagonal tower erected in 1891, during the Victorian era when exotic creations were in vogue. The Pagoda, as it is commonly known, is being renovated so that Baltimoreans can once again enjoy the magnificent view from the top.*

For those who love the water, Baltimore County is a big playground, with 173 miles of tidal shoreline and plenty of freshwater recreation. On the open waters of the Chesapeake Bay, water skiing **(left)** and sailing are favorite pastimes; the Glenmar Nighthawk Series **(above)** out of Middle River is one of the most popular racing series on the bay, held on Wednesday evenings from May through September. For avid fly fishermen, Gunpowder Falls **(right)** offers some of the finest trout fishing east of the Mississippi. This catch-and-release stream is well stocked with brown, rainbow, and brook trout. Since the 1940s the cold waters of Beaver Dam **(far left)** have offered thousands of Baltimoreans relief from summer's heat waves. This massive pit in Cockeysville, mined for more than a century, has yielded some of America's finest building marble — including two monuments to George Washington and 108 columns for the U.S. Capitol in Washington, D.C.

Emotions run high at the last opening day **(right and following pages)** at Memorial Stadium, Baltimore's tenth and longest-lived ballpark since professional baseball took root here in 1865. Since 1954 Memorial Stadium has hosted thirty-eight seasons of Orioles action, attended by nearly fifty million fans. During the past three decades, the Birds have won three World Series, six American League pennants, finished first in their division eight times, and posted the league's best won-lost percentage. Of late, the Orioles have been in a rebuilding phase, injecting young talent like pitcher Ben McDonald **(left)**, the first player selected in the 1989 free agent draft. Major League Player of the Year in 1991, shortstop Cal Ripken, Jr. **(below)** is the team's ironman and living legend, playing more consecutive games at any one position than any other player in baseball history. Relief pitcher Mark Williamson **(below)** is besieged by fans with pens.

Maintaining a Maryland tradition of well over three centuries, the huntsman for the Green Spring Valley Hunt **(right)** prepares to head out with his pack of hounds in pursuit of the red fox. Contrary to popular belief, the object of this imported English sport is not to kill the fox; the sport derives from chasing the wily fox over varied terrain, filled with challenging obstacles. The ever-alert red fox is infrequently seen, yet very common in suburban Baltimore. Early European settlers, frustrated with the indigenous gray fox, which can simply climb a tree to end the chase, imported red foxes to satiate their love of the sport.

Since its first running in 1894, the Maryland Hunt Cup has become a favorite Baltimore rite of spring. This classic four-mile race of twenty-two jumps, set over the picturesque countryside of Worthington Valley, is acknowledged as the toughest timber steeplechase on any continent. At at height of 4'9", the third fence **(above)** is nicknamed the "Union Memorial Jump," in honor of the hospital that has treated some of its casualties. The Hunt Cup is not only the grand finale of Maryland's point-to-point circuit, it hosts one of the year's premier social gatherings, where spectators dressed to the nines stage elegant tailgating parties. A victorious Sanna Neilson **(below)** celebrates after winning on her maiden voyage over the Hunt Cup course in 1991, an exhilarating race in which she defeated her father, a three-time winner himself.

Baltimore glows in the national spotlight during the Preakness Stakes, run each May at Pimlico Race Track as the second jewel of the Triple Crown racing series. Though crowds may approach 90,000 spectators, only a fraction will actually see the race among the nation's fastest three-year old thoroughbreds. The most celebrated of all the traditions that surround the Preakness is the Winner's Circle ceremony **(above)**, where a blanket of black-eyed susans (actually 1,500 daisies hand-colored to resemble Maryland's late-blooming official state flower) is presented to the 1990 winner Summer Squall ridden by Pat Day — along with the Woodlawn Vase, the most valuable trophy in American sports. The Preakness is also a renowned social spectacle, attracting everyone from the exuberant, let-it-all-hang-out youth of the infield, to the Preakness Village patrons — the social, political, and corporate elite who are treated to a fine day at the races.

Billed as the fastest game on foot, lacrosse in Maryland is more than a traditional sport embraced by schools, colleges, and clubs; it is a cultural icon so entrenched that it has spawned a movement to have it usurp jousting as the official state sport. As the lacrosse capital of the world, Baltimore is home not only to the most consistently excellent team in the history of collegiate lacrosse — the Johns Hopkins University Blue Jays **(left)** — but to the new Lacrosse Foundation National Headquarters and Hall of Fame Museum, also located on the Homewood campus. At a Lutherville springtime league **(above)** warriors as young as six years learn the basics of this action-packed contact sport, distinguished as North America's oldest sport. Women's lacrosse **(right)**, played under slightly different rules, also generates intense action, as evidenced by the pair of Roland Park Country School teammates drilling before a game.

Following pages: Windsurfers race their ultra-colorful sailboards during a Baltimore Area Boardsailing Association regatta. Numbering 625 members and growing, BABA is one of the country's largest windsurfing clubs, drawing members from throughout the Mid-Atlantic region. In addition to offering public clinics and sailboard rentals, BABA stages regattas and beach parties for its members at Gunpowder Falls State Park (Hammerman Area) and Rocky Point Park in Baltimore County.

Above: *A peregrine falcon, fondly named Blythe, feeds her clutch of four on a ledge of the 37-story USF&G building in downtown Baltimore. Since nesting activity began here in 1978, nearly fifty eyases have been raised successfully under the care of several breeding pairs. Through the work of the Peregrine Fund Project at Cornell University, this endangered species has been reintroduced as a breeding species east of the Mississippi. By the 1960s peregrines had disappeared from the region, mainly due to the presence of the pesticide DDT (now banned) in the food chain, which weakened their ability to reproduce.*

Right: *A bird bander examines the skull of a northern cardinal, netted in the woodlands of Green Spring Valley. This program is one of numerous nature activities conducted by the Irvine Natural Science Center, located on the campus of St. Timothy's School in Baltimore County. In 1975 the center was established to promote environmental awareness and responsibility; Irvine makes learning about nature fun with interesting programs like stream monitoring workshops and moonlight hikes through owl country.*

Left: *A Krider's hawk displays his magnificent plumage for school children at the Carrie Murray Outdoor Education Campus in Leakin Park. Within this 1,200-acre wilderness park, teeming with wildlife, the Carrie Murray Center rehabilitates injured birds and cares for a variety of non-releasable birds of prey, which are used with other animals for educational programs. The center is named after the mother of former Baltimore Oriole Eddie Murray, who provided the funding.*

Above: At Ladew Topiary Gardens visitors are treated to the unusual art of topiary — the sculpting of shrubs and trees into ornamental shapes — in addition to a spectacular variety of vibrant flowers. This 22-acre site within the tranquil countryside of Monkton was originally the home of Harvey S. Ladew, an avid fox hunter and gardener. Inspired by English topiary displays, Ladew developed his own creations between 1929 and 1971 without professional assistance. In 1976 he bequeathed for public enrichment his beloved gardens and country manor house, noted for its exquisite rooms filled with English antiques.

Left: Sherwood Gardens bursts into color in late April and early May with a splendid mix of flowers, trees, and shrubs. Covering some six acres, the gardens are famous for their tulips; approximately 80,000 bulbs, representing dozens of varieties, are planted annually. Sherwood Gardens was created in 1927 as the private hobby of John W. Sherwood on his estate in the North Baltimore neighborhood of Guilford. Following his death in 1965, the garden was purchased by the Guilford Association, which maintains the property in cooperation with the City of Baltimore.

The Pride of Baltimore II *sails as a unique representative of the citizens of Maryland, promoting business and cultural links to trading partners the world over. On her most recent voyage, the* Pride II *sailed some 30,000 nautical miles during an eighteen-month whirlwind tour of Europe, visiting twenty-seven countries and forty port cities, including London* **(above)**. *Launched at the Inner Harbor in April 1988, the* Pride II *is a traditional topsail schooner, modeled after the famed nineteenth century Baltimore clippers, swift vessels whose design and construction helped to establish Baltimore as a preeminent port city. As merchant ships and privateers, these schooners played a key role in the maritime history of the young republic, especially during the War of 1812, when they captured or sunk nearly 1,700 British merchant ships.*

Life on board the Pride of Baltimore II is extremely challenging, and her die-hard sailors would not have it any other way. At an overall length of 157′3″, she is sailed by a professional crew of twelve; duties include steering and navigation, monitoring the weather, adjusting the sails, and inspecting the boat for various mechanical and safety concerns. In addition, Pride II requires constant maintenance: scrubbing, sanding, varnishing, and repairing her many surfaces. Unlike her predecessor, the Pride II is licensed to carry passengers, providing adventurous souls an opportunity to step back in time and assist the crew in the ship's operation. In port, crew members become apprentice ambassadors, answering questions and giving tours for the public and special receptions sponsored by Maryland-based companies, tour and convention officials, and the Maryland Port Administration.

Above: *World-class cyclists shoot across the streets of Baltimore during the 1990 Tour de Trump, America's answer to the world-renowned Tour de France. This ten-day international cycling extravaganza, featuring more than 120 of the biggest names in amateur and professional cycling, passed through six Atlantic seaboard states, covering some 1,000 miles.*

Right: *Legends recapture the glory days of tennis at the Baltimore Country Club in Roland Park during the Maryland National Tennis Classic in 1989. This one-time nostalgic event offered three days of men's singles and doubles, showcasing the talents of such greats as John Newcombe, Roy Emerson, Frew McMillan, and Pancho Gonzales.*

Left: *Swift J-44s light up the Patapsco River during the Cadillac Columbus Cup — Baltimore's premier international yachting event since 1989 — hosted by HarborView Marina & Yacht Club. This week-long series of fleet (all eight boats race together) and match (a round-robin of one-on-one pairs) racing features eight world-class skippers, including America's Cup challengers and Olympic medalists and contenders.*

Of the more than 700 species of birds commonly found in North America, over 300 have been identified in the Baltimore area alone. Among the more interesting species are **(clockwise from bottom left)** the black-crowned night-heron, American kestral, American goldfinch, red-bellied woodpecker, and the osprey **(right)**. The abundant bird life of Baltimore is mainly due to geography. As a Mid-Atlantic state, Maryland provides refuge to an interesting mix of southern and northern species. Also, the Chesapeake Bay (the nation's largest estuary) is a major wintering ground for a host of migratory North American waterfowl. Greater environmental responsibility, such as the protection of wetlands along the Patapsco River, has also helped to attract more birds to the area.

Left and right: Polo fans are treated to explosive action by the Maryland Polo Club in Monkton. Though this prestigious equestrian sport is the world's oldest stick-and-ball game, the Maryland Polo Club, formed in 1986, is a relative newcomer to the scene. From June through October, the club hosts games and tournaments — both on the dirt surface of the Elkridge-Harford Outdoor Arena, and on grass at the Timonium Fairgrounds and the new field at Ladew Topiary Gardens.

Below: An eventer charges through the water jump — appropriately named "Sheila's Splash" — during a two-day competition at Jackson's Hole Farm in Baltimore County. Taking on a variety of formats, venues, and skill levels, the sport of eventing is essentially a multiphase competition which tests the endurance and versatility of horse and rider. The Jackson's Hole Trials involve three tests: dressage, cross-country, and stadium jumping.

History is made on April 6, 1992 — the first Opening Day at Oriole Park at Camden Yards — as the Baltimore Orioles

Cleveland Indians and a sellout crowd stand for the National Anthem. The Orioles won 2-0 on this grand day.

Baltimore celebrates Oriole Park at Camden Yards as the most heralded downtown attraction since Harborplace and the National Aquarium. Completed at a cost of $106.5 million in 1992 as the new home of the Baltimore Orioles, the 48,041-seat stadium combines state-of-the-art facilities with old-fashioned architecture and an asymmetrical natural grass playing field, evoking the elegance of early twentieth century ballparks. Integral to this plan is the preservation and restoration of the historic Camden Station **(above)** — crowned in 1992 with side cupolas and a tiered clock tower — and the massive B&O Railroad warehouse — eight stories tall and more than 1,000 feet long. This landmark provides dining facilities and office space for the Orioles. In every detail, from the vintage scoreboard **(left)** and uniforms of the ushers **(right)** to light rail transit for fans **(below)**, Oriole Park at Camden Yards is a welcomed walk down memory lane, paving the way toward a new era for Baltimore.

215

Above: Week-old Welch foals test their wobbly legs, which may someday be called upon to pull a carriage or chase a fox. Baltimore County is one of the most prolific horse breeding counties in the United States, with nearly 150 thoroughbred farms alone. Other popular breeds include Arabians and quarter horses.

Left: The autumnal blaze over Rolling Mill Farm's main driveway, lined with dozens of ancient maple trees, makes for one of Baltimore County's most dramatic seasonal spectacles.

Glimpses of professionals at work illustrate a glorious sporting legacy in Baltimore. The "golden arm" of Johnny Unitas **(left)** fires a pass during the USF&G Legends Bowl I in 1989, a 20th anniversary flag football rematch of Super Bowl III between the Baltimore Colts and the New York Jets. Local talent Pam Shriver **(above left)**, one of the world's top doubles players, works out in preparation for an upcoming tournament. The Baltimore Skipjacks **(above right, in white),** farm team for the Washington Capitals, face off at the Baltimore Arena during an American Hockey League contest. High-scoring Dominic Mobilio **(below)** of the Baltimore Blast sets up against the St. Louis Storm at the Baltimore Arena, where the Blast thrilled Major Soccer League fans from 1980 to 1992.

Above: The pristine watershed of Loch Raven Reservoir is a mecca for fishermen, who test their skills in pursuit of pike, catfish, bass, and other species. A fishing center is open from March to October, providing boat rentals, fishing licenses and tackle and bait. Loch Raven, formed in 1881 by damming the Gunpowder Falls, is the oldest of the three county reservoirs which currently supply Baltimore City. Though swimming is not allowed, Loch Raven is one of the area's most popular recreation spots, with a number of hiking trails through woodlands rich in wildlife and wildflowers.

Left: Oregon Ridge provides year-round adventure with 1,035 acres of unspoiled Piedmont woodlands in the heart of Baltimore County. Favorite activities offered by this increasingly popular park include cross-country skiing, swimming, hang-gliding, hiking, and picnicing amidst the harmony of the Baltimore Symphony Orchestra during the summer concert series. In addition, the Oregon Ridge Nature Center brings visitors close to nature through special exhibits and programs relating to the flora, fauna, and natural history of the area.

INDEX

ACKNOWLEDGMENTS

Though only one name appears on the cover of this book, I could not have assembled *Baltimore* without the contributions of numerous people who have worked with me on this project. My sincere thanks to you in helping me capture the best of Baltimore:

My parents, Bob and Shiny Evans, for their assistance in the production of the book, and for their tireless efforts towards making Middleton Press a success

Betsy Hughes, for her thorough scrutiny of the text of Baltimore, and for her unyielding enthusiasm for my career

Judie Deakins, for her help in the daily operations of Middleton Press

Carleton Jones, for sharing his insightful words on Baltimore

Eli Renn and Fred Kaufman of Baltimore Color Plate, for furnishing a magnificent set of color separations

Scott Jamieson, Alan Abrams, Diane Dickey, George Shifflett, and the rest of the Garamond Pridemark staff for their enthusiasm and commitment to printing this book to the highest standards

Jeanie Will, Laurie Will, and the wonderful employees of Art Comp and Design Company, for an excellent job on the pre-press work for Baltimore

Steve Hammett of Advantage Book Binding, for his efforts to insure the completion of a well-bound book

Jack Warns and his staff at True Color Professional Lab for their friendly service and genuine interest in this project

Last, but not least, the scores of people who helped me in my effort to photograph Baltimore; without all of the boat and plane rides, press passes, keys to get onto rooftops, etc., I would not have been able to capture these moments. I cannot thank you enough.

TECHNICAL NOTES

All of the photographs in this book were made with five 35mm Nikon cameras - either the FE2 or F3 models. Sixteen lenses were used - all but one of them Nikkor - ranging from a 16mm f/2.8 fisheye to a 600mm f/4 ED-IF telephoto. However, a majority of the 294 images in this collection were made with just two lenses - a Tokina f/2.8 28-70mm zoom and a Nikkor f/2.8 80-200mm AF zoom. One of my favorite lenses is the Nikkor 28mm f/3.5 perspective control lens, which corrects for the distortion that occurs when wide angle lenses are used from a tilted position. Concerning film, eight types were exposed to handle a variety of lighting challenges. Towards the beginning of this three-and-a-half-year project, I started to use Fujichrome color slide film, primarily due to the improved color saturation. Currently, my film of choice is Fujichrome Velvia (ASA 50), which I shoot whenever the lighting is adequate. Several high-speed negative films were used to record performances under existing light. Kodak Ektar 1000 and Fujicolor 400D yielded the best results. Other equipment included Nikon MD-4 and MD-12 power winders, a Nikon 1.4x teleconverter, Bogen tripods and monopods, and a Metz 45 CT-3 flash.